CREATING
COMMUNITY

ANDY STANLEY
AND BILL WILLITS

Multnomah® Publishers *Sisters, Oregon*

CREATING COMMUNITY
published by Multnomah Publishers, Inc.

© 2004 by North Point Ministries, Inc.
International Standard Book Number: 1-59052-396-2

Unless otherwise indicated, Scripture quotations are from:
The Holy Bible, New International Version © 1973, 1984 by International Bible
Society, used by permission of Zondervan Publishing House.

Multnomah is a trademark of Multnomah Publishers, Inc.,
and is registered in the U.S. Patent and Trademark Office.
The colophon is a trademark of Multnomah Publishers, Inc.

Printed in the United States of America

For information:
MULTNOMAH PUBLISHERS, INC.
POST OFFICE BOX 1720
SISTERS, OREGON 97759

Library of Congress Cataloging-in-Publication Data

Stanley, Andy.
    Creating community / Andy Stanley and Bill Willits.
        p. cm.
    ISBN 1-59052-396-2
    1. Group ministry—Baptists. 2. Small groups—Religious aspects—
Baptists I. Willits, Bill. II. Title.
    BV675.S74 2005
    253'.7—dc22

                                2004019834

06 07 08 09 10—10 9 8 7

CONTENTS

Part IV
Connection Needs Simplicity

Part V
Processes Need Reality

Acknowledgments

No book like this is the work of just one person. It involves the collective efforts of many who have passion for the subject matter (and pity for the author). God has allowed me to share this life and this project with some very creative and enjoyable people. Some share my last name. Some I work with. Others are personal friends. But all have been amazingly supportive to me during the writing of this book.

Special thanks go to my fellow North Point leadership team members, Julie Arnold, Rick Holliday, Lane Jones, Reggie Joiner, David McDaniel, and of course, Andy Stanley. Many of the concepts and ideas expressed in these pages are simply applications of principles developed during our numerous discussions. You are the most gifted and fun group of leaders on the planet. It's a blast doing life and ministry with you.

To the North Point Group Life team, especially Steve Giddens, Fran LaMattina, Jason Malec, Mitzi Miller, Stephen Redden, Al Scott, Sean Seay, and John Woodall. You had as much to do with the work contained in these pages as anyone. You are an amazing group of leaders. I am beyond thankful that

God has allowed me to work with such talented and Christlike friends.

Our unsung heroes, the people who make these concepts a reality every week, deserve special kudos. They are the numerous volunteer group leaders and assimilators who call North Point their church home. Your passion and commitment to Christ and to your groups inspire and challenge us all. We are learning much from you. Thanks for making community a way of life for so many people in Atlanta.

Much of what it means to live in community we have learned from our current and former community groups. We have laughed a lot, challenged one another, cried together, and seen God at work. We have had good times and hard times, but we have experienced the love of Christ in tangible ways because of your faithfulness to Him and to His church.

There are certain people who have given extra effort toward this project. Thanks to Jan Woodruff, my assistant, for keeping my life and ministry straight during this writing season. I know you have had to carry an extra burden, and I am grateful. Thanks to Dawn Hurley in Andy's office, who has been extremely helpful in editing the manuscript. Thanks also to Michael Colwell and John Woodall for your help with the discussion questions. And thanks to Justin Craig for keeping me out of the tall weeds theologically with your helpful research.

Every person is the product of many influences. So is every church. No one has had greater influence on the small-group movement, or the development of our small-group ministry, than Bill Donahue, Russ Robinson, and the team at Willow Creek. Bill mentored us in our early days and has been a great source of encouragement along the way. Thanks, great friends.

To our friends at Multnomah—Don Jacobson, Kevin Marks, Doug Gabbert, Brian Flagler, David Webb, and Kristina Coulter—thank you for partnering with us and believing in this project. Your lives, ministry, and commitment to excellence bless us. And the community culture you have created at Multnomah inspires us.

Creating Community would never have been written without the support of my *favorite* small group, my family.

T, I wouldn't have made it without your love and belief in me. I am so thankful to experience life with you. Thanks for filling in the gaps while I was preoccupied, cheering me on when the going got toughest, and for reading and rereading the manuscript. Your insights were extremely helpful, reminding me once again why you are the best author in our home. I am so proud of you and thankful to be your husband.

Bailey, thank you for being so understanding while Daddy was busy writing. I am a blessed man to call you my girl. You have asked me frequently, "When are you going to be done with your book?" I can finally say, "It's done." Ready to go out on another date?

To my mom and dad, I am grateful and proud to call you my parents. You have taught me by example a lifelong commitment to friends and community. My generation can learn a lot from you.

To my in-laws, Bus and Carmen Ryan, thank you for your encouragement and support throughout this entire process, especially by loaning me your "summer place" to do much of my writing.

Most of all, I want to say thanks to God for connecting me into life-giving community through His Son, Jesus Christ, more than thirty years ago.

Bill Willits

THINKING GROUPS

In 1993, Sandra and I joined Bill and Terry Willits, along with three other couples, to form a small group. At the time I was working for my dad at a Baptist church. There was no small-group ministry in the church. Like most Baptist churches, adult education happened within the context of Sunday school, and as a staff member working with high school students, I was not able to attend an adult Sunday school class. Sandra and I felt that something was missing.

We had lots of friends. We both had older people in our lives to whom we looked for advice and accountability. We weren't having marriage problems. Everything was great. But we were keenly aware that nobody was tracking with us as a couple. We weren't praying together with any other couples. We weren't sharing our lives with other couples going through our same season of life. And for some reason I still don't completely understand, we decided this was something we needed.

I shared our frustration with Bill. He and Terry had some of the same concerns about their own experience as a couple. So we decided to form a small group. We each invited other couples to join us. Then one week before we were to begin, I met a family at church that was new to the area and needed a place to plug in. What I didn't know at the time was that the husband was not a believer. More on that later.

What's important to understand at this point is that our group was not part of a church program; this was not a means to any preconceived end. We were just a handful of couples who sensed a need for community. We didn't use the term *community* back then. But looking back, that's exactly what we were missing. We all sensed a need to bring a layer of structure and intentionality to our otherwise random and unstructured friendships. We needed a predictable environment. We needed to "do life" together with other couples.

During the year we were together, several remarkable things happened. We celebrated the birth of a child, while at the same time locking arms with another couple in the group as they struggled with the pain of infertility. One man lost his job. Another couple almost lost their marriage. And toward the end of that year, we wept together as the gentleman I mentioned earlier shared that he had finally crossed the line of faith.

Those twelve months marked us. Sandra and I have been in a small group ever since. Our lives have gotten much busier. The demands of ministry have become heavier. Our three children require more time than ever before. But being in a small group is a nonnegotiable for us.

We are about to begin our eleventh group. We have two couples from our former group and three couples we met through our boys' involvement with baseball. Most of these new couples have been attending North Point Community Church for less than a year and cover the gamut in terms of spiritual maturity. Sandra and I can't wait to get started.

CREATING A CULTURE

When Bill Willits and I first talked about creating this resource, we asked ourselves, "What do we have to say about groups that is unique?" Several things came to mind, but the primary thing that bubbled to the surface during our conversation was the notion that North Point really does have a small-group "culture." The small-group program is not an appendage; it is not a program we tacked onto an existing structure. The small group is part of our lifestyle. We *think* groups. We organize everything with groups in mind, and everything points to group life. In many ways, group life drives what we do—and do not do—as an organization.

The only numeric goal we have ever set for our ministry was in the area of small-group participation. Why? We really do believe that life change happens within the context of intentional relationships. And since our mission as a church centers on life change, we decided to lean the entire ministry in the direction of groups.

Whenever I talk to senior pastors about their small-group ministries, I always ask about their personal small-group experience. The majority of the time—and I mean the *vast* majority of the time—it turns out that the pastor is not actively participating in a group. At that point I say something rude. I think it is hypocritical for a pastor to champion something he isn't willing to participate in himself.

Meanwhile, the small-groups director is standing there giving me imaginary high fives. He or she knows what many senior pastors don't: Groups don't really impact a local church until they become part of a church's culture. And that begins with senior leadership.

MEET YOUR GUIDE

Bill has done the lion's share of the writing for this project, and rightly so: He lives in the trenches of group life. One of North Point's six original staff members, Bill is the architect of our groups ministry. Our shared small-group experience back in 1993 ignited a passion in him to create a small-group culture in our church, and he has done exactly that. Under his leadership this area has flourished to the point that we now have more than seven thousand adults participating in small groups.

An entrepreneur and strategist, Bill led the charge to develop a closed-group model at North Point. I don't know of any other church that had embraced this concept before Bill began championing it. His leadership and courage enabled us to develop closed groups that multiply. We were told that it couldn't be done and that we were foolish to try. Bill proved the skeptics wrong.

Bill has developed a plan that our staff and volunteers are able to run and run well. As the church has grown, Bill has continually reengineered our groups ministry to keep up with the demand and to follow his vision to involve every member and attendee in a group.

Many fine books have been written on the topic of small groups. I've probably read most of them. What makes this book different is the fact that you can hop on a plane and fly to Atlanta, Georgia, and experience everything contained in these pages. The principles and environments discussed are a daily reality for those of us who call North Point Community Church home. For that reason, I believe *Creating Community* has the potential to revolutionize *your* small-group ministry, as well as your small-group experience. Enjoy!

Andy Stanley

Part

I

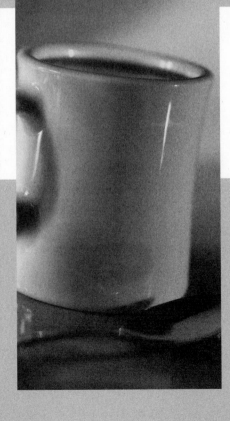

PEOPLE NEED
COMMUNITY

CHAPTER ONE

A CULTURE CRAVING RELATIONSHIP

Most mornings, after hitting the snooze button, I do what a lot of people do and faithfully visit my local Starbucks for a cup of the day's fresh brew. I begin to crave that first sip as soon as I walk out the door and get into my car. I've become such a regular that the Starbucks employees know my name, and I know theirs. Starbucks has become more than a purveyor of caffeine for me; it has become a part of my daily routine.

One day, while adding the necessary additives to make the product "my" coffee, I saw a card that caught my eye. If you are an occasional patron of Starbucks, chances are you've seen it, too. It's a card promoting career opportunities at Starbucks. No, it didn't intrigue me because I was looking for a job. What made the card stand out was the title. The card read, "Create Community. Make a difference in someone's day." Since the subject of community not only intrigues me but also employs me, I immediately picked it up. On the back of the card it went on: "When you work at Starbucks, you can make a difference in someone's day by creating an environment where neighbors and friends can get together and reconnect while enjoying a great coffee experience."

. Interesting, isn't it? Starbucks sees itself in the business of doing more than selling a premium cup of coffee. Starbucks believes part of its corporate purpose is to create environments that connect people so meaningfully that it changes the quality of their lives. Hmm. Sounds familiar.

According to the Starbucks website, what they are selling is the "Starbucks experience." And we're buying. Revenues for the upcoming fiscal year are expected to be in excess of five billion dollars, and Starbucks expects to open thirteen hundred new stores globally next year. Most recently, Starbucks was named among the ten most trusted global brands.[1] Not bad for a company whose primary commodity is beans. Starbucks is using coffee to promote connection. That's a good thing because the company knows we are a culture craving relationship.

TRADING SPACES

Several years ago, my wife, Terry, who is an interior designer, read something about home construction that caught her eye. The article she was reading noted that most architects currently design homes intentionally to promote privacy and seclusion, not connection. Not so back when life was simpler and commute times were nonexistent. Back then homes were constructed with front porches, so when people took evening walks or afternoon drives, it was commonplace to "run into" your neighbors sitting on their porch. One thing usually led to another, and before long, you were invited to sit with them and enjoy casual conversation and a cold beverage. People actually took the time for one another and saw value in this spontaneous interaction. Talk time on the porch was a way of life. As one writer has observed, "The American front porch further represented the ideal of community in America. For the front porch existed as a zone between the public and the private, an area that could be shared between the sanctity of the home and the community outside. It was an area where interaction with the community could take place."[2]

Welcome to the twenty-first century. Retreating from the busyness and intensity of work life, we come home, put the garage door down, and escape. Not outside to the openness of our front porch, but inside to the TV in our living room. And if we go outside, it's not to the porch on the front of our house, it's to the deck on the back of our house. The harsh truth is that after a long, hard day, and perhaps a crowded commute, we don't want to see *more* people. We want to get away from them! The last thing we want to do at the end of a day is to have one

more conversation, be forced to make one more decision, or fulfill one more request. So we shun unplanned interactions by
hiding. Our goal is to avoid people—and what they potentially
want from us—at all cost! And cost us it does, because the avoid-
ance approach comes with a price tag.

**Our goal is to avoid people at all cost—
and cost us it does.**

ALL THE LONELY PEOPLE

George Gallup has said, "Americans are among the loneliest
people in the world."[3] In the midst of busy lives, overcommitted
schedules, and congested cities, we feel alone. Although we drive
on overcrowded freeways to catch overbooked flights and sit in
jam-packed airplanes, we live in isolation. But how can that be?
Most of us are mobbed with people. Lots of them.

Most of us live around a lot of people, work with a lot of
people, and attend sporting events with a lot of people. Because
of the size of most fitness centers today, we even work out around
a lot of people! Sound familiar? As one writer has observed,
"Today more than three-fourths of the American people live in
metropolitan areas, and more than two-thirds of those live in

suburbs."[4] And many times those suburbs are made up of mammoth subdivisions, some bigger than small towns. And if you live in my area of the country and don't like the people you live or work around, you have the option of getting on a plane and visiting 80 percent of the country's population within two hours!

Having access to people isn't the issue for most of us. So why the loneliness?

Debbie is a single woman in her late twenties. She has great leadership gifts and a promising career. Her commitment to her job has made her a rising star in her company. Senior management is beginning to notice her. But working six days a week has also kept her from having a life outside of work. For the most part, Debbie doesn't get out much. There's just too much to do. When she's not working, she is renovating her loft. Her parents are worried about her. The girl who once had several inseparable friends has drifted away from those relationships. "That's the price of working for a Fortune 500 company," she tells them.

Besides, she is with people all the time. At work, at her gym, and at her church, people are everywhere. Debbie is surrounded by people. True, she doesn't really know any of them, and they don't know her. Which was fine, until recently. Doing life alone is taking its toll: Debbie is beginning to feel alone, even in crowds.

For almost ten years, my wife and I worked predominantly with singles in their twenties and thirties in a metro area with over one million singles. If that describes your stage of life,

Atlanta is a great place to live. And North Point is a great place to attend church. More than one-third of our congregation is made up of single adults. We host a weekly Bible study called 7:22, where more than twenty-five hundred college students and singles show up every Tuesday night. While involved in this ministry, I served alongside some of the most amazing followers of Christ on the planet who were exploiting their current season of life for God's purposes. But it wasn't rare for me to talk with some in this same group who were experiencing exactly what Debbie experienced. Even though they were living in a large city, working at a successful company, and attending a large Bible study, they felt alone. The volume of their acquaintances wasn't the problem. They were acquainted with many people, but they were known by none. And this issue was not just the result of their marital status. Many couples will tell you they experience the same thing. Being married does not exempt someone from the emptiness associated with isolation.

We are a culture craving relationship. In the midst of our crowded existence, many of us are living lonely lives. We live and work in a sea of humanity, but we end up missing out on the benefits of regular, *meaningful* relationships. Let's look next at why God is so concerned about this unhealthy reality in our culture.

"Americans are among the loneliest people in the world." —George Gallup

CREATE YOUR COMMUNITY

1. Describe a meaningful relationship you've had. What made it so significant?

2. Why are people today so lonely?

3. Do you think people really want community? Why?

4. What do you think people are looking for?

5. Describe the last time you had a meaningful interaction with a neighbor.

CHAPTER TWO

IT'S NOT ALL GOOD

I have an amazing nephew named Van. For several years we lived three doors down from his family's house, so we got to spend a lot of time together. In fact, his diaper was the first one I ever changed. While we have a lot of fun memories of Van and his sister centered around holidays and family gatherings, my favorite times with them have been when they spent the night with us. Not having kids of our own, we tried to make every visit to our house fun and memorable. That usually included a lot of laughter. And a few trips to the mall.

Today, Van is fifteen years old, plays a sweet guitar, and has an authentic relationship with Christ. We are very proud of the man into which God is shaping him. Like most guys his age, Van is well acquainted with slang. Some of his conversations with friends are quite entertaining. If you have a teenager, chances are you know what I mean. If I ask him how he's doing, he is likely to say, "It's all good." When I ask him if he wants something, and he doesn't, he says, "I'm good." I guess the words *fine* and *no* are no longer part of a teenager's verbiage.

As we pointed out in the last chapter, it's not "all good" when it comes to the way most of us are living. That's because we were never meant to live in a state of functional isolation. We were created to be relational beings. Granted, we all have varying relational needs based on our wirings and temperaments; but the truth is, none of us was meant to live alone, away from meaningful connection. As one writer put it, "I have never known anyone...who was isolated, lonely, unconnected, had no deep relationships—yet had a meaningful and joy-filled life."[5] And yet, as we discussed, that's the way many of us have chosen to live. We live life *around* many people, but we experience life deeply with none. It's no wonder so many of us feel alone and isolated, experiencing what one observer has called "crowded loneliness."[6] But that's not what God originally intended.

THE ORIGINAL PLAN

In Genesis 1–2, we read the Creation account and how God planned for us to "do life." If you haven't read it in a while, take a fresh look. It is an amazing reminder of God's endless capacities. With little effort, but amazing creativity, God creates the heavens and earth and everything in it. The breadth and depth of what God was able to get done in six days is very sobering for any results-oriented, type A person. Talk about cranking it out! But then again, there is no one like Him. He's God.

In the midst of His creative bonanza, a recurring phrase appears. In fact, six times after God creates something the text says, "and God saw that it was good." From light to livestock, the assessment of His efforts is the same: It is good. He is pleased. Things are as He intended them to be. Then on the sixth day, humankind comes on the scene. The culmination of God's creativity has arrived. God is so pleased by this latest creation, that as He assesses all His efforts over the previous six days, His appraisal changes. With His latest addition, the things He had created are no longer just good. They are now *very* good.[7] God's prized creation had tipped the scales. With the addition of humankind, God awards His five-star rating.

Then the unexpected happens. After explaining in more detail His design and intentions for man, God says, "It's not all good." Up to this point, everything was as it was intended. But in Genesis 2:18, God says something isn't right. He says, "It is not good for the man to be alone." For years, many of us have heard this passage quoted in the context of marriage, and rightly so. But I believe the implications go beyond an affirmation of the marriage relationship. At its core, this is a statement about the importance of our connecting well with others, the marriage relationship being the most profound illustration of that reality.

John Ortberg has made a helpful observation on this passage:

What is striking is that the Fall has not yet occurred. There is no sin, no disobedience, nothing to mar the relationship between God and man. The human being is in a state of perfect intimacy with God. Each word he and God speak with each other is filled with closeness and joy; he walks with God in the garden in the cool of the day. He is known and loved to the core of his being by his omniscient, love-filled Creator. Yet the word God uses to describe him is "alone." And God says this aloneness is "not good."

Sometimes in church circles when people feel lonely, we will tell them not to expect too much from human relationships, that there is inside every human being a God-shaped void that no other person can fill. That is true. But apparently, according to the writer of Genesis, God creates inside this man a kind of "human-shaped-void" that God Himself will not fill.

No substitute will fill this need in you for human relationship. Not money. Not achievement. Not busyness. Not books. Not even God Himself. Even though this man was in a state of sinless perfection, he was "alone." And it was "not good."[8]

I can hear the chorus now. "Thanks for the reminder. If there is one thing I know, doing life alone is not good. Actually, it stinks." And you would be right. When our "human-shaped-void" is not filled, when we live life alone in isolation, it is not good. And for good reason.

ISOLATIONITIS

When we aren't in meaningful relationship, we suffer natural consequences, whether we realize it or not. Several relational maladies tend to come our way.

Lost Perspective

When we live in isolation, we can easily lose perspective on life. That's because there is no objective voice calling us toward balance. Our lows tend to be lower, and our highs tend to be higher. Our point of view becomes clouded and things tend to seem worse (or better) than they really are. Simple decisions can appear bigger than life and decision making can become more impulsive when we don't have others to point us back to "truth north."

And lest we forget, we can lose the perspective that, as believers in Christ, we are in a battle. We can forget that we have a very real enemy and that he plays for keeps. We can lose sight that "our struggle is not against flesh and blood"[9] and that our enemy's most successful strategy is to isolate us so he can attack and destroy us. Sheep are never attacked in herds. Sheep are attacked when they become isolated from the rest of the flock.

Sheep are never attacked in herds—they are attacked when isolated from the flock.

Fear of Intimacy

People who don't have meaningful relationships tend to fear intimacy more. If you've never had close friendships, then you're going to tend to be more fearful of that kind of relationship. People who fear intimacy think that if others really get to know them, they won't like them. So they would rather stay disconnected than risk rejection. By the way, that's why I believe one of the best preparations for marriage is participating in a small group. If a person has learned to be intimate and honest with a few friends before they get married, they will have less reason to fear intimacy after they are married. Their track record for transparency will give them confidence as they enter into this new season of life.

Selfishness

Disconnected people tend to be more selfish. Isolation breeds selfishness. If the sum total of a person's life is defined by his schedule, his agenda, his needs, and his desires, chances are good he is suffering from a good dose of selfishness. Over time, a disconnected person becomes self-absorbed. He gives in to one of the fatal by-products of disconnection: self-centeredness. When that happens, life is lived and seen through a very narrow lens.

Poor Health

People who live life alone are at much greater risk of sickness and poor health than their connected counterparts. John Ortberg, in his book *Everybody's Normal Till You Get to Know Them*, refers to a study on relationships that tracked the lives of seven thousand people over nine years:

> Researchers found that the most isolated people were *three times more likely to die* than those with strong relational connections. People who had bad health habits (such as smoking, poor eating habits, obesity, or alcohol use) but strong social ties lived *significantly longer* than people who had great health habits but were isolated. In other words, it is better to eat Twinkies with good friends than to eat broccoli alone.[10]

Actually, in Atlanta, we would choose Krispy Kreme donuts over Twinkies any day, but you get the point. Strong relationships pay huge dividends, even toward our health.

Clinical psychologist Dr. Henry Cloud references two reports that communicate similar findings. Their conclusions affirm the value of meaningful connection: "A person's ability to love and connect with others lays the foundation for both psychological and physical health. This research illustrates that when we are in a loving relationship, a bonded relationship, we are growing. When we are isolated, we are slowly dying."[11]

Living life without meaningful connection is not good because it's not what God intended for us. Isolation tends to bring with it devastating relational sicknesses. But it's also not good because we were created for relationship. Living life alone does not accurately reflect the One whose image we bear.

Living life alone does not accurately reflect the One whose image we bear.

JUST LIKE HIM

We have been blessed with a five-year-old daughter named Bailey. All kids are special to their parents, but I choose to believe Bailey is extra special—what dad worth his salt doesn't think so?—because of how long we had to wait for her. Like more and more couples every year, we took a lot longer to start a family than we had once anticipated. About thirteen years longer, to be exact. But now that we have our incredible gift, we are enjoying the pleasures of parenting.

One of the joys (and challenges) of Bailey's fun personality is that she is a very active little girl. She is constantly busy and enjoys the company of her many friends. At five years old, there does not *appear* to be an introverted bone in her body. She loves to talk; she loves to sing; she loves to play; she loves to perform. And like any extrovert, she loves to do these things with people around. At a recent party one of our friends, remarking on her outgoing personality, said, "It is so amazing. Bailey is just like Bill. Their personalities are so much alike."

The truth is, we were all created in the likeness of our Father. Our heavenly Father. And God is a relational being. As God the Father, God the Son, and God the Holy Spirit, He is three persons in one. In Genesis 1:26, God said, "Let *us* make man in our image" (emphasis mine). The God who desires to have a relationship with all humankind has always known meaningful relationship. Always. And don't miss out on what the passage goes on to say: "So God created man in his own image" (v. 27). Just as He exists in meaningful relationship, so are we to exist in this quality of relationship as well. The need for it is part of our genetic makeup. God is a relational being and He created His prized creations, you and me, with the *need* for significant relationship as well.

That's why, from God's perspective, living life alone is "not good." It's not good because it's not how He created us to live.

Alone and *isolated* were never to be used to describe His children. It's not good because we were created with a deep need for rich and meaningful connection with other people. Without it, we don't reflect the image of the One who created us. And without it, bad things happen, like lost perspective, fear of intimacy, selfishness, and poor health.

Henry Cloud says it well: "God created us with a hunger for relationship—for relationship with Him and with our fellow people. At our very core we are relational beings." He goes on to say, "The soul cannot prosper without being connected to others."[12]

So what is God after in His desire to move us toward these kinds of connected relationships? Pass the Krispy Kremes, turn the page, and we'll find out.

CREATE YOUR COMMUNITY

1. Can someone live a joy-filled life in isolation from others?

2. Describe a time when you were not living in meaningful relationship. What were some of the consequences?

3. Do you agree with the statement that there is a need inside of us that not even God Himself will fill?

4. Several consequences were mentioned for people who live in isolation. Which consequence can you identify most with?
   a. Lost perspective
   b. Fear of intimacy
   c. Selfishness
   d. Poor health
   e. Other

5. How does living in community reflect the image of God?

CHAPTER THREE

THE DIVINE COMMUNITY

We all have hopes and dreams. We all have things we would like to do or see accomplished in our lifetimes. It could be to have the ideal job, run a marathon, become financially free, have the "perfect" kids, live in a nicer home, start your own business venture, or go on a dream vacation. We all have dreams. What are yours?

Do you know that God has a dream for you and me? Some of us may think that God only cares about what we will do, whom we will marry, or what we will accomplish with our lives. Like any loving father, God dreams about all the things that will ultimately bring His children happiness, satisfaction, and joy. He dreams about the things that He knows will bring fulfillment to our lives. Because of this, I believe one of God's biggest dreams for us is authentic community—the kind of meaningful relationships that are best characterized by oneness with Him and with one another.

One of God's biggest dreams for us is authentic community.

THE POSSIBLE DREAM

We read of God's dream for us in the words of Jesus as recorded in John 17. This is really the recording of a prayer. As Jesus moves toward the cross, He prays not for Himself, but for those He will leave behind. With His life almost over, He discloses what's closest to His heart, what's foremost on His mind. In their book *Building a Church of Small Groups,* my friends Bill Donahue and Russ Robinson have provided a helpful insight:

> It is sometimes said that when someone faces death, one's conversation reveals his or her deepest passions, hopes and dreams. That's why we go out of our way to honor dying wishes. In his final hours, Jesus gives us clues to His chief concerns.[13]

It's obvious from Jesus' prayer that His focus was on His followers. His primary concern was with the depth of relationship the disciples would experience with one another. Notice His words: "I will remain in the world no longer, but they are still in the world, and I am coming to you. Holy Father, protect them by the power of your name—the name you gave me—so that they may be one as we are one."[14]

So that they may be one as we are one. The significance of this statement cannot be overstated. Jesus is praying that His disciples—the men who for three years had disappointed Him and misunderstood Him and would ultimately abandon Him (in other words, human beings like you and me)—would experience something amazing. He prayed they would experience the same quality of relationship with each other that Jesus had been enjoying as part of the Trinity since before the beginning of time. To understand the significance of this, we need to explore what this quality of relationship really looks like.

Throughout the Scriptures, the Trinity—God the Father, Son, and Spirit—is seen expressing a unique, affirming kind of relationship toward one another. They are seen enjoying one another (see Genesis 1:26), encouraging one another (see Matthew 3:17), supporting one another (see John 14:25), loving one another (see Mark 9:7), deferring to one another (see John 14:10), and glorifying one another (see John 17:1). If you get the picture that they have an ongoing mutual admiration society, you're right. What's not to admire about actions that are so selfless? What's not to love about expressions of servanthood and support? These types of relationships breathe life into our souls.

As Ortberg notes:

> This is why the experience of authentic community is so
> life giving. We are taking our place in fellowship with
> Life himself. When I am in isolation, I am lonely. When
> I am in community, I experience what might be called
> "fullness of heart." The human heart is forever empty if it
> is closed in upon itself. In community—the divine com-
> munity especially—a heart comes alive.[15]

Jesus' prayer was that the disciples would experience these kind of life-giving relationships with one another. The kind that make our hearts come alive. The kind that can only come from God Himself.

AN OPEN INVITATION

It would have been understandable had Jesus' prayer been only for the disciples. After all, they had spent three years together, walking the breadth of Galilee and Judea. But His prayer wasn't just for them. John 17:20–21 makes that clear.

> "My prayer is not for them alone. I pray also for those
> who will believe in me through their message, that all of

them may be one, Father, just as you are in me and I am in you. May they also be in us so that the world may believe that you have sent me."

Jesus' invitation to life-giving relationships was also for those who would come to faith through the disciples, which includes us! How's that for amazing grace? Jesus' prayer was that all His followers would experience the kind of meaningful relationships with each other that the Trinity has always experienced. That qualities like mutual encouragement, support, love, deference, and honor would characterize our relationships with one another just as they do with them. That was His prayer and that is His dream.

As important as it is for each follower of Christ to give and experience this unique kind of relational life, the benefits go beyond ourselves. They influence a watching world. Notice Jesus' concluding words to verse 21: "so that the world may believe that you have sent me."

Do you feel the weight of that statement? Jesus is saying that the credibility of His life and message in the eyes of unbelievers is dependent upon the way we as His followers relate with one another. Somehow their belief and our behavior are connected. It's as if Jesus is saying that unbelievers are just waiting to believe, but the question is, Will they see us relating in this magnetic, irresistible way? Remember these earlier words from Jesus?

"A new command I give you: Love one another. As I have loved you, so you must love one another. *By this all men will know that you are my disciples,* if you love one another."[16]

Do you see how high the stakes really are? Do you grasp why we can't settle for anything less than Jesus' dream for community? The credibility of the gospel is at stake!

As Francis Schaeffer rightly said, "Our relationship with each other is the criterion the world uses to judge whether our message is truthful—Christian community is the final apologetic."[17]

"Christian community is the final apologetic."
—Francis Schaeffer

THE CHURCH IN COMMUNITY

In this first section, we have emphasized the fact that people need community. We are a society living in isolation, seldom enjoying the benefits of meaningful relationships. We live and work around a lot of people, but most of us have chosen to do life alone. This is certainly not what God has in mind. We were cre-

ated by a relational God with relational needs for significant connection. And when we don't connect well, bad things follow.

The kind of connections we need are more than casual.
Casual connections aren't life-giving. They can't provide what
Jesus dreams for and what He died for. They can't provide the
kind of oneness with God or oneness with each other that makes
the world take notice. The kind that God uses in the hearts of
people. The kind that transforms lives. Only the church in community can display that kind of relational oneness. Only God's
Spirit unleashed through His Body can make that kind of difference.

Randy Frazee says it well:

The development of meaningful relationships where
every member carries a significant sense of belonging is
central to what it means to be the church. This is a God-
ordained gathering of people that is so strong that even
"the gates of hell will not overcome it."[18]

That is what God has called the church to be about: creating
environments where authentic community can take place.
Building relational, transforming communities where people are
experiencing oneness with God and oneness with one another.
Communities that are so satisfying, so unique, and so compelling that they create thirst in a watching world.

So how do we go about creating this kind of community?

What are some of the things we need to consider to make God's dream a reality? What are some strategies that allow Jesus' prayer to be experienced by more and more people? Let's take a look.

God has called the church to create environments where authentic community can take place.

CREATE YOUR COMMUNITY

1. Do you agree that one of God's dreams for His people is community? Why is this so important?

2. What role has community played in your faith journey?

3. What are the characteristics of community that make it attractive to those outside the faith?

4. Do you agree with the idea that community is the "final argument" for Christianity? Why or why not?

5. Why should the church intentionally foster community? Why can't we just rely on the casual connections we make at church?

Part
II

LEADERS NEED
CLARITY

CHAPTER FOUR

CLARIFY THE GOAL

The first year of North Point Community Church saw us meeting at the Galleria Convention Center in Atlanta. Not the typical meeting place for a new church, but our beginnings were anything but typical. We had a lot of people attend from the beginning. We started with a staff of six. Our services were held every other Sunday night. Our first worship band was an audio track. And we took two months off when the 1996 Summer Olympics came to town.

From time to time people ask us how to plant a church from scratch. The truth is, we really don't know much about it. Our first years were anything but typical.

WHAT'S THE POINT?

I'll never forget coming to the Galleria one Sunday afternoon to help with setup. The Galleria is located at the intersection of two major freeways in Atlanta, I-75 and I-285. As you might expect, the Galleria has a state-of-the-art electronic marquee advertising its venue and the group that is currently using its facility. Thousands of cars pass by the convention center every day, so the impact of the marquee from an advertising and awareness point of view is very high.

As I drove into the facility that night, I was amused by what I saw. On the marquee were these words:

"No Point Church"

Not "North Point Community." Not "North Point CC." Not even "North Pt. CC." But "No Point Church." Ouch! The sign engineer obviously couldn't get North Point Community Church all on one screen, so he took some creative liberties.

As you would imagine, this electronic faux pas became the joke of the night. We had a lot of fun with it. After welcoming people to "No Point" church, Andy reminded us that this was an issue with a lot of churches. They had lost their point, and we needed to make sure that we stayed on mission so we didn't follow suit. The signage that night made us laugh, but it also provided a subtle reminder for us to stay focused on what God had called us to do.

So what *is* the point? What's the point of your church? What's your mission? What's your goal?

What is the point of your church?

TIME TO DREAM

When North Point first started, we had time and lots of it. Holding services every other Sunday night for three years gave us a lot of extra time together as a leadership team, time most staffs never have the opportunity to enjoy. Before you get a picture of half days and frequent golf outings, you need to know that we were all busy. We each had areas to oversee and teams to lead. We were all focused on enlisting volunteers or creating ministry environments for students, singles, and families. Some of us were developing processes for membership and care, finding property, and designing our current building. And on our Sundays off we visited other churches.

We were busy. We just didn't suffer from the "tyranny of the urgent" most church start-ups experience. Every day didn't seem like Sunday. This unique period gave us valuable time to dream, discuss, strategize, and pray. It put us into a rhythm of meeting weekly and prioritizing regular off-site planning times. And this was before we even had a site to be off of! As we look back on those early days, we can see they were a gift from God. They were crucial to the direction we would take and the decisions we would ultimately make.

THE BIG THREE

Early on, Andy led us in a discussion centering on three critical questions. We didn't come to a decision on any of them in one meeting. It was actually a series of interactions that led us to our conclusions. This was not a fast and pain-free process, but then again, most important conversations rarely are. Acquiring clarity on these three questions proved to be vital to the development and implementation of our mission, strategy, and values.

WHAT DO YOU WANT PEOPLE TO BECOME?

The first question we set out to answer was, *What do we want people to become?* In other words, what do we want the result of our efforts to be? When it's all said and done, what do we hope happens in the lives of the people we influence? Answering this question was critical to the others because it provided us with something important—clarity of *mission*.

Most churches seem to fall into one of two categories.

The Skill-Based Church

Some churches could be classified as *skill-based churches*. Their primary focus seems to be on people becoming proficient and effective in certain skills. As a result, these churches direct their attention toward training and development by adding more and more options to their educational efforts. They add more classes, more seminars, more courses, more conferences, more training, more of everything. After all, more is better, right? What they forget is that adding more opportunities immediately dilutes the effectiveness of any one of the other established options. Having too many options weakens the impact of the things that are most important. And everything is not equally important.

The Bible-Knowledge Church

Another group of churches could be called *Bible-knowledge churches*. Their core purpose is to help people become biblically literate. They prioritize their programming efforts around teaching people the contents of every book in the Bible. From their worship services to their classes, from adults to children, they want people to have a thorough understanding of the Scriptures. On the surface, this seems to be a very noble goal. What church that believes in the divine inspiration of the Bible doesn't want its people to be biblically literate? The challenge with this approach is in its assumptions. Many times churches with this view assume that the books of the Bible are equally important. They are not. They are equally inspired, but they are not equally applicable.

Before you pick up a stone, let me explain. It is very important to us that a five-year-old understands that God created her and loves her so much that He gave His Son to die for her.[19] This is a foundational truth that will transform her life. Her eternal destiny is dependent upon her response. However, her understanding of events like King David's sin with Bathsheba[20] or that God directed Joshua and the nation of Israel to kill the people of Ai[21] is not important to us at her age. Are they true? Absolutely. Are they helpful in introducing a five-year-old to God? I don't think so. These stories are not age-appropriate, and they can easily confuse or scare her.

You need to know I am all for people becoming competent around certain skills and knowledgeable about the Scriptures. I believe both play an important role in a person's spiritual development. Competence in areas like relational evangelism is key for people to become effective partners with God. Biblical literacy is important for people to become lifelong self-learners of the Scriptures and doers of the word.[22] But in and of themselves, I would suggest they aren't the goal. They aren't the bull's-eye on the target. They can be helpful, but they shouldn't be the things used to define what we want people to become.

Clarifying what you want people to become will ultimately define your church's mission.

MISSION DEFINED

The good news is our mission has already been defined for us! Jesus' parting words in Matthew 28 made it very clear:

> "Therefore go and make disciples of all nations, baptizing them in the name of the Father and of the Son and of the Holy Spirit, and teaching them everything I have commanded you."

Jesus made it clear that our mission is to make disciples. Jesus was saying that as we go through the normal stuff of life—as we go to work, interact with our friends, and do all the things we normally do—our purpose is to relationally connect with people in such a way that it encourages them to follow Christ.

LEADING PEOPLE

Taking our cue from Matthew 28, we at North Point answered this first question. We want people at North Point to be *growing* in their relationship with Jesus Christ. Spiritually speaking, we want them to be moving the ball down the field. What that means is that wherever people may be on the spiritual continuum—skeptic, new believer, returner, growing believer, etc.—we want them to be continuing to take steps forward in their faith relationship with Christ. That may involve their investigating their faith for the first time. It may have to do with their

making a difficult decision in a current relationship, or with rais-
ing their children, or with stewarding their finances. Whatever
the area, we want people to be demonstrating greater faith and
living in greater surrender to the will of their heavenly Father.

We're not concerned if people are not at the same place on
their spiritual journeys. We simply want to influence people in
such a way that they keep making progress on their journeys. So
North Point's mission statement is pretty easy to figure out. Our
mission is to lead people into a growing relationship with Jesus
Christ.

But the real question is what do you want the people in your
care to become? Is it clear? Is it well known? Clarifying what you
want people to become will ultimately define your church's mission.

CREATE YOUR COMMUNITY

1. Why is it important for an organization to have a clearly defined mission statement?

2. What is the mission of your church?

3. How would you define a disciple?

4. What do you want the people you influence to become?

5. How has this been communicated to them?

CHAPTER FIVE

DEFINE SPIRITUAL MATURITY

The second question we asked ourselves was, *What do we want people to do?* If answering the first question answered the *What?* for us, then answering this second question answered the *How?* In other words, how are people going to become what we want them to become? What are the things we want them to tangibly do to get there? As we answered this question, it forced us to clarify our understanding of spiritual maturity.

NOT JUST A PLAN

Over the years I have noticed that some people seem to equate spiritual growth with the accomplishment of a process or plan.

They seem to believe that mature Christ-followers are those who have endured the equivalent of spiritual boot camp. If you have successfully undergone a regimen of classes, seminars, and prescribed activities, you are perceived as mature. If you finish the list, you have arrived. You are discipled. Project completed. This perspective assumes that spiritual maturity comes at a point in time—namely, when the process or curriculum has been completed.

I am all too familiar with this curriculum approach to spiritual maturity and what it produces. I helped develop one of these processes myself several years ago at another church. Back then I called it my "track to spiritual growth." To be honest with you, it was more like a "pathway to spiritual burnout." I illustrated my process using a funnel. The top of the funnel was wide, but with each passing step the circumference of the funnel narrowed. Adhering to this process (or so I thought) would result in the goal—a more fully discipled participant.

The first step in this profound process was for people to attend the Sunday morning worship service. Easy enough. After that, they were to attend a Sunday school class that would provide them with a relational connection and another opportunity for someone to speak at them. The third step in this "funnel of fun" was for them to break out into a sub-group, where the care and prayer needs of the class would be addressed. The fourth step was for them to take advantage of the plethora of discipleship and equipping opportunities we provided on a regular basis.

Lastly, we wanted them to find a place of personal ministry where they could use their spiritual gifts. Needless to say, this track was not user-friendly and frustrated the participants and the point leader (me). It was developed with the right goal in mind, but it produced something different; worn-out, well-informed graduates were the only fruit born from this life-draining model.

A curriculum or a series of classes may be helpful, but they shouldn't be considered the determinants for spiritual growth. They may help people become better informed about their faith, but they don't automatically lead people to maturity.

WHAT DO YOU WANT PEOPLE TO DO?

If completing plans or consuming curriculums isn't what we're after, what do we want people to do? How are people going to become what we want them to become? What demonstrates a growing relationship with Jesus Christ? Jesus' words in Matthew 22 give us the answer. In this familiar passage, Jesus was asked to identify the greatest commandment in the Law of Moses. He replied:

> "'Love the Lord your God with all your heart and with all your soul and with all your mind.' This is the first and greatest commandment. And the second is like it: 'Love your neighbor as yourself.' All the Law and the Prophets hang on these two commandments."[23]

At the risk of oversimplifying, it seems clear that Jesus is saying that loving God and loving your neighbor is what it all comes down to. He says everything written in the Scriptures up to that point could be reduced to those two commands. In other words, the activity and instruction of God for all time can be summed up in two things: loving Him and loving others. That's it. These two activities give evidence of a person's spiritual growth and maturity.

It's important to note that the love Jesus speaks of in this passage is not a one-time kind of love. The verb He uses implies continual action. Our love for Him and our love for our neighbors are to be repeatedly and continually expressed.

This passage implies that spiritual growth is a process. Maturity is measured by demonstrative growth in our love for God and for others. It is not a completed program or the acquisition of a skill, but a continual expression of love in our vertical relationship with God and our horizontal relationships with one another.

Saying spiritual maturity is a point in time is like saying physical fitness is a point in time. It's like saying because we were once fit and understand what is required to stay in shape, then we will remain fit. But we all know that physical fitness is not something we achieve once and for all. It's something we must continually pursue. It requires regular exercise and a healthy intake of the right diet. It's not a point in time, but a continual pursuit. Likewise, spiritual growth is meant to be a continual pursuit of our relationship with God and others.

At North Point, we have divided "loving our neighbor" into two categories: those in the faith and those outside the faith. So we have defined spiritual maturity as continual progress in three vital relationships: a person's relationship with God, with other believers, and with unbelievers. So what do we want people to do? We say it this way: We want them to grow in their intimacy with God, community with insiders, and influence with outsiders.

Saying spiritual maturity is a point in time is like saying physical fitness is a point in time.

Intimacy with God

The Bible records God's deep love and His passionate pursuit of all humankind. And because He desires an intimate relationship with every one of us, we believe the mark of a maturing follower is that they are *continually* pursuing an intimate relationship with Him.

After all, intimacy in any relationship doesn't just happen. It requires regular relational deposits. Imagine the state of a marriage where the husband and wife did not put any time or attention into their relationship. It might be characterized by a lot of things, but intimacy would not be one of them. Our relationship with God is no different. An intimate relationship with

Him is not something we arrive at; it is something we continually pursue. And as we do, we enjoy the benefits and demonstrate the marks of a maturing follower.

Community with Insiders

Recognizing people's need for meaningful connections and the reality that *sustained* life change takes place best in the context of intentional relationships, we want people to be growing in community with other believers. We believe that a person who is continuing to mature in his faith is meaningfully and regularly connecting with other believers. Since the human propensity is to drift, we need one another for mutual encouragement and accountability. The words of Hebrews 10 come to mind:

> Let us consider how we may spur one another on toward love and good deeds. Let us not give up meeting together, as some are in the habit of doing, but let us encourage one another.[24]

Maturing believers are people who are growing in community with other believers, spending time together, encouraging one another, and supporting one another.

Influence with Outsiders

Because God has invited us to partner with Him in the process of evangelism, we at North Point want people to prioritize relationships with their unbelieving friends for the purpose of seeing these friends come to faith. We call it our "invest and invite" strategy: We encourage people to *invest* in the lives of their unbelieving friends and then *invite* them at the appropriate time to one of our relevant environments, where these guests will be encouraged in their spiritual journey.

Many of our most spiritually vibrant attendees started out as disconnected, uninterested neighbors, coworkers, and friends. Then one day, a friend or neighbor invited them to visit one of our ministry environments and they experienced God in a fresh, relevant way. Nothing motivates believers (or small groups) more than when they see God using them to bring someone to Him. So we believe one of the marks of a maturing believer is that they are pursuing influence with those outside the faith.

To us, whether you are eight years old or eighty, a spiritually maturing person looks the same. He is not someone who has completed a plan or curriculum. He is not someone who has simply acquired more truth. A maturing believer is someone who is continuing to grow in these three distinct relationships.

—·—

What do we want people to become? We want them to grow in their relationship with Jesus Christ. What do we want people to do? Continually pursue three vital relationships—intimacy with God, community with insiders, and influence with outsiders.

So what do *you* want people to become? More importantly, what do you want people to *do*? Answering these two questions is critical to gaining clarity in defining your mission and how you hope to accomplish it.

CREATE YOUR COMMUNITY

1. How does a person become spiritually mature?

2. How would you describe a growing relationship with Christ?

3. Do you agree that it's important to understand spiritual growth as a process rather than as a point in time? Why?

4. Are each of the three vital relationships equally important in the growth process?

5. What does your church want people to do? How has this been clearly communicated to them?

CHAPTER SIX

DECIDE WHERE PEOPLE GO

For the past thirteen years, the Braves major league baseball team has been the pride of Atlanta. (Before then was another matter.) Because their broadcasts reach a nationwide audience on "superstation" WTBS, the Atlanta Braves have been dubbed America's Team. Since 1991, they have won eight divisional titles and five National League championships. In 1995, they won the World Series.

Every spring, these boys of summer begin their preparation for the upcoming season with one end in mind. They show up at spring training with one destination in sight: postseason play. From the front office to the bat boys, from the coaches to the players, everyone's goal is the same. It is not enough for them to just "play ball" and take home a paycheck. Success for the Braves is measured by playing in October.

We have discussed two of the three critical questions that helped bring directional clarity to North Point Community Church. Both questions—*What do we want people to become?* and *What do we want people to do?*—were critical in helping us define and set into motion our mission. The last question we needed to answer was *Where do we want people to go?*

WHERE DO YOU WANT PEOPLE TO GO?

Intentionally or by default, people are going to end up somewhere. One way or another, people are going to arrive at a destination. The question is, will it be where we want them to be? Will it help them best do what we want them to do?

Answering the question *Where do we want people to go?* allows you to clarify the "win" for your organization. Regrettably, many churches are not clear on what a win looks like for them, so they don't know how to go about achieving the win. Using a Little League analogy, my friends and colleagues Andy, Reggie Joiner, and Lane Jones discuss this dilemma in *7 Practices of Effective Ministry*:

> Some organizations are like Little League batters. If they just hit the ball anywhere, they get excited and feel good about what they've done. It doesn't really matter if they

get on base or if what they do actually gets them where they want to go. They are just trying to hit the ball somewhere. They're not thinking about home plate and the steps to get there.

They go on:

Unfortunately, churches have a reputation for doing ministry without an end in mind. They build as many rooms as possible to reach as many people as possible. They start new ministries to target a variety of issues. They create countless programs to meet the growing needs of those who are attending. It all makes sense. It all seems right. It even feels productive. But there is no overall strategy and no runners are moving home. The question they should be asking is not *Are we hitting the ball?* but rather *Are we getting closer to home plate?*[25]

So where do you want people to go? Have you decided what home plate looks like for you or your church? Or, like some, have you created multiple home plates?

Have you decided what home plate looks like for your church?

HEADING TO CLASS

One approach is to assign people to a class that targets their age group or season of life. It's a good system for connecting people, unless there are competing options.

When I led the adult Sunday school charge in a former church, we wanted adults to ultimately end up in an age-appropriate Sunday school class. At least, we who were leading the Sunday school wanted them there. This is where it got fun. The discipleship leaders wanted these people to attend a discipleship class. The membership leaders wanted them to attend a new members' class. The counseling leaders wanted them to attend a counseling class. For the staff, it was frustrating; for the participant, it was confusing.

For many churches, a class is the ultimate destination in their strategy. It's where they want people to go.

IMPROVING THEIR SERVE

For other churches, the destination is a service team. They ultimately want people moving in the direction of a ministry or service group impacting the community or an area inside the church.

It goes something like this: "God has gifted each person uniquely with a spiritual gift, and those gifts are to be employed for His glory and for the building up of His body. The best thing we can do is to help people discover and start using their gifts in a place of service."

While in the ministry trenches together, it is believed that the group will experience community. For these churches, a service team is used as a pathway to community.

NEW MEMBERS SEMINAR

There are churches where the preferred destination is a doctrinal seminar for new members. They want to make sure that everyone is on the same page theologically, so their desire is to move attendees toward this kind of experience. They make it clear that they want people to go to their membership class or weekend retreat.

There is not a right or wrong approach. Any one of these can work. One may work better than another at creating opportunities for meaningful relationships to develop, but the critical issue is that you need to have clarity about where you want people to go. What's most important is that you clarify your organizational "win" and let the people around you know what it is.

THERE'S NO PLACE LIKE GROUP

As we discussed this question at North Point, it became clear that our approach would be to move people into small groups. From children to adults, we wanted people's destination to be the same: Everyone, regardless of age or season of life, would be encouraged to move into a small group.

We wanted to send a consistent message about something we believe very passionately. We have found that the best place for sustained life change to occur is within intentional relationships. And like many church leaders, we feel that the best place for encouraging intentional relationships is in a small group. While we believe other approaches can work, we think the small-group model works best.

We'll discuss our small-group approach more completely later, but for us, the answer to where we want people to go is clear. We're unanimous about where we want people to go: to a small group.

So what do we want people to become? People growing in their relationship with Jesus Christ. What do we want people to do? Pursue three vital relationships. Where do we want people to go? Into a small group.

From children to adults, we want people's destination to be the same.

CRYSTAL CLEAR

A scene from the Tom Cruise movie *A Few Good Men* comes to mind. Cruise plays Lt. Daniel Kaffee, a naval attorney assigned to provide legal defense for two enlisted men charged with the mysterious death of a fellow soldier. Through the course of the investigation it becomes clear to Cruise that these two Marines were following orders to discipline the soldier by giving him a beating, but never meant to kill him. In order to pin the responsibility on those who gave the order, Kaffee makes the risky move of calling Col. Nathan Jessup (played by Jack Nicholson) to the stand, knowing that if he is not successful, his inappropriate questioning of a superior officer could be grounds for a court-martial.

During their exchange the young lawyer asks the hardened colonel if it was absolutely clear to the men under him that the soldier was not to be touched. "Crystal," replies the highly decorated Marine. As Lt. Kaffee continues to push, the colonel grows weary of his authority being called into question and unleashes a string of questions aimed at his accuser, making sure the young lawyer feels the gravity of the situation.

"Have you ever spent time in an infantry unit, son? Ever served in a forward area? Ever put your life in another man's hands, asked him to put his life in yours? We follow orders, son. We follow orders or people die. It's that simple. Are we clear?"

Kaffee responds, "Yes, sir."

"Are we clear?" Jessup seeks to hammer his point home.

The young lawyer, feeling the weight of the words and struggling to do the right thing, pauses. If he continues this line of questioning, it could cost him his career. If he doesn't press further, two men will alone bear the shared sin. Steeling himself, he responds.

"Crystal."

Becoming crystal clear on what you are trying to do is critical for any group or organization. Without clarity an organization becomes pointless. Getting clear begins when we answer three important questions:

What do we want people to become?

What do we want them to do?

Where do we want them to go?

Answering these questions is vital for gaining clarity of mission and strategy. These are issues all leaders need to be clear on. Crystal clear.

CREATE YOUR COMMUNITY

1. Using the Little League analogy, what is wrong with simply putting the ball in play?

2. Where does your church want people to go?

3. What are the advantages and disadvantages of having only one home plate that everyone agrees on?

4. Does your church have any competing systems?

5. Do you believe that sustained change occurs best in intentional relationships? Why or why not?

Part
III

CHURCHES
NEED
STRATEGY

FIND YOUR WORD

Something comes to mind when the name of your organization comes up. Hopefully, whatever comes to mind is positive, but your church is associated with *something* in the eyes of your community. What comes to mind when you read the names of the following well-known companies?

Coke
Chick-fil-A
Starbucks
Bayer
Hershey
Federal Express

Each of these companies has strong ties to a single corresponding word and for good reason. For Coke, it is obviously their cola. Coca-Cola is one of the world's most recognizable brands and the company is best known for its original Coke. Chick-fil-A is not known for inventing the chicken, but they *are* known for inventing the chicken sandwich. And a great one it is. Starbucks and coffee are almost synonymous these days. The Bayer Company and aspirin have been linked together for years. They may sell other products, but they are *known* for aspirin. Hershey and chocolate are inseparable. And when Federal Express is mentioned, most people immediately think of overnight shipping. Apparently, the U.S. Postal Service does too—there's now a FedEx box outside most post offices.

Several years ago, our leadership team read Al Ries's book *Focus*. In it, Ries talks about the importance of an organization finding the word they want used to describe themselves. He says it is an organization's "fundamental strength," more valuable than anything else. After reading this particular chapter, we discussed what we wanted North Point's word to be. After all, we knew we were going to be associated with *something* when our name came up.

When people think of your organization, what is the word they will associate with it?

When people think of your organization, what is the word you hope they will associate with you? Something is going to come to mind. What do you want it to be?

In this section, I want to discuss a church's need for strategy. Clear, simple, compelling strategy. Strategy that helps the church accomplish its mission. If clarity around mission is the first step, then executing a strategy is the next. Finding your organization's word is a valuable step in arriving at an effective strategy.

KNOWN FOR SOMETHING

Over the years, I have heard churches described in several different ways. When their names come up in conversations, some specific quality is usually quickly attributed to them.

Evangelistic

Some churches are known as evangelistic churches. Because of their preaching ministries and programming, they are known for challenging people to an immediate decision for Christ. Featuring regular gospel sermons and midweek visitor follow-ups, they are known for their evangelistic fervor.

Worship

Some churches are known as worship churches. More than anything, they want to connect people's hearts to the heart of God through passionate corporate singing and ministry. So they devote a significant amount of time to this purpose. While prepared, they do not feel compelled to share a message if it gets in the way of what they sense they need to do.

Doctrinal

Some churches are known as doctrinal churches. They are passionate about regularly and systematically equipping their attendees in the foundational elements of faith and their denominational distinctives. Doctrinal understanding and conformity is important to these kinds of churches, and, as a result, this is often how they are perceived in the community.

Recovery

Some churches are known as recovery churches. They spend an enormous amount of energy on helping people recover from life's disappointments, challenges, and sorrows. From their preaching services to their recovery groups, they focus their efforts on healing people's emotional and spiritual wounds. People in pain and crisis can find a helpful home in this kind of church.

Service

Finally, some churches are best known as service churches. They feel it is their responsibility to be "salt and light" by meeting the material needs of those around them. These churches are known especially for their work among the poor and the disconnected of society.

The fact that a church may be known by one of these descriptions doesn't mean that's *all* they are known for. It simply is what they are *best* known for in their communities.

DETERMINING OUR WORD

Knowing people would be thinking something about North Point when our name came up, we settled on "our" word. The word we hoped people would associate with us was *relational*. We wanted people to think of us as a *relational church*. We came to this conclusion because we believe it is a word that describes the balanced Christian life. First, the invitation God makes to us is to enter into a *relationship* with Him through His Son, Jesus Christ. As we discussed previously, we believe that a growing, maturing Christian is someone who is pursuing three vital *relationships*—intimacy with God, community with insiders, and influence with outsiders. In the pursuit of these relationships, some come to faith, people worship, truth is taught, the broken recover, and material needs are met.

But the word *relational* also captures how we want to operate the church. We want to do ministry in the context of relationship *in* communities, not *on* committees. And there is a difference. A committee is a group of individuals that gather together for the sole purpose of accomplishing a task. This is fine because we, too, want to get a lot done, but it's incomplete. We want to operate in a way where our staff and volunteer teams are highly successful in their roles, yet are experiencing a level of community. After all, if the church is championing the value of community, it needs to be modeled by its leaders. That's why our leadership team has met together every Monday morning since our inception. And it's why we spend a week together with our spouses at an off-site retreat every year. That's why our entire staff gathers weekly to share stories and celebrate what God is doing in our midst and pray together.

We want to operate in a relational way that values people as much as their organizational contributions. It might not always be the most efficient way to function, but for us, we have found it to be the most effective. So *relational* became the word we want to be known by.

What about you and your organization? What is the one word you want used when people talk about you? Again, what's most important is that you land *somewhere* because something *will* come to mind when the people in your community describe you. Fairly or unfairly, a word will come up. What do you want it to be?

Finding your word can be an integral part of strategy development. It can help you determine what you want to be known for, as well as those things you don't. It will not only describe what you value, but as we have found at North Point, it can influence how you operate. Churches need strategy. Finding your word is a great place to start in defining what your strategy will be.

CREATE YOUR COMMUNITY

1. When people think of your organization, what one word comes to mind? Why?

2. What are the benefits and disadvantages of being known in this way?

3. What word do you want people to think of?

4. Would this word affect how your organization operates?

CHAPTER EIGHT

CHOOSE YOUR STRATEGY

Once you've defined your goal and then found your word, it's time to decide how you are going to get to your goal. It's time to settle on a delivery method. It's time to choose your strategy.

The dictionary defines *strategy* as "a plan of action...intended to accomplish a specific goal."[26] A strategy is simply the method you use to accomplish your mission or achieve a goal.

THE FIRST CONSULTANT

One of the earliest and most familiar strategies is found in Exodus 18, where Moses is serving as an overworked and underappreciated judge for the people. In fact, he is working himself to death! The Scripture says that when his father-in-law saw all he was doing, he confronted Moses:

"What is this you are doing for the people? Why do you alone sit as judge, while all these people stand around you from morning till evening?"

Moses answered him, "Because the people come to me to seek God's will. Whenever they have a dispute, it is brought to me, and I decide between the parties and inform them of God's decrees and laws."

Moses' father-in-law replied, "What you are doing is not good. You and these people who come to you will only wear yourselves out. The work is too heavy for you; you cannot handle it alone. Listen now to me and I will give you some advice, and may God be with you. You must be the people's representative before God and bring their disputes to him. Teach them the decrees and laws, and show them the way to live and the duties they are to perform.

"But select capable men from all the people—men who fear God, trustworthy men who hate dishonest gain—and appoint them as officials over thousands, hundreds, fifties and tens. Have them serve as judges for the people at all times, but have them bring every difficult case to you; the simple cases they can decide themselves. That will make your load lighter, because they will share it with you. If you do this and God so commands, you will be able to stand the strain, and all these people will go home satisfied."[27]

Wise words from the first recorded organizational consultant. Select capable people, train them, empower them, focus your efforts, and experience a longer, more enjoyable life. A great strategy. It's simple to understand and easy to implement.

A great strategy is simple to understand and easy to implement.

THE NORTH POINT STORY

God was leading us to a strategy for North Point long before we realized it. As Andy mentioned in the Introduction, about twelve years ago he and I were on staff together at his dad's church, helping lead the educational ministry. We were busy, our schedules were full, and we knew a lot of people, but there wasn't a group of people with whom we were walking through life in a meaningful way. We were two guys with exciting jobs, married to incredible women, but living fairly isolated. So Andy and

Sandra found two couples, and Terry and I found two couples, and we started our first small group.

Some great things happened during our time together, as was mentioned. Families expanded and the kingdom expanded. For us, the group came together during a very difficult season in our lives. While we were going through infertility, I was leading the couples ministry (aka the baby factory). Our group became a lifeline for us as we navigated through this painful chapter in our lives. I am convinced that we would not have made it had it not been for the support and grace extended to us by the group.

Our group experience was so beneficial that after a year, Andy and I wanted other people to experience these same benefits. So we divided the group, added people, and the story of our first group has continued to multiply itself to this day. As we look back on twelve years of group life, we are grateful we took the plunge.

WHY GROUPS AT NORTH POINT?

Our personal experience was one of the most compelling reasons we chose to pursue a small-group strategy at North Point. Our heritage and familiarity were more aligned around a Sunday school model, but we chose small groups because of the depth, satisfaction, and life change that had occurred in our group.

What we soon discovered is that sustained spiritual growth is not well nurtured by an environment where people simply sit in rows, listening to messages in complete anonymity. Sustained growth takes place where people are personally challenged and encouraged in their relationship with God and others. This is especially true when the challenges of life occur, and eventually those challenges come to everyone.

But there are also a number of other reasons why small groups were a better fit for us than were other effective approaches like ABF groups (Adult Bible Fellowship) or traditional adult Sunday school classes.

Groups Support Our Evangelism Strategy

Our small-group approach supports, rather than competes with, our "invest and invite" evangelism strategy. We encourage our attendees to invest in the lives of unbelievers and then invite them to a relevant ministry environment. One of our most effective environments for adults is our worship service. Small groups allow our attendees the flexibility to bring people to services without missing their personal connection time.

We have also found that some unchurched people are more open to connecting in a home than they are willing to visit a church. Some want to *belong* before they are willing to *believe*. They want to "taste and see" if it is good before they are willing to jump in.

Some people want to belong before they are willing to believe.

Groups Decentralize Church Leadership and Care

Our groups strategy gives us many shepherds in our church, not just a few. This allows us to spread out the leadership and care responsibilities to the places where it happens best, with the people to whom others have connected well. We have found that people are naturally cared for best by those who know them best—those with whom they are walking through life.

As we involve more people in leadership, this enables us to utilize a broader range of spiritual gifts. Within each group, those with hospitality gifts can host; those with the mercy gifts can coordinate care; and those with leadership gifts can lead the group.

Groups Enable More People to Serve

This has also been a huge win for North Point. It takes about eighteen hundred volunteers a week for us to do what we do on a Sunday morning. From our production team to our kids' small-group leaders, it requires a lot of manpower for us to produce the worship service and park and care for all those who come through our doors. Our groups strategy has freed up adult attendees from choosing whether to serve on Sunday morning or attend a class. This would not be the case if we had a competing classroom system.

Our strategy has freed up members from choosing whether to serve or attend a class.

Groups Help Develop Authentic Community

We'll discuss this point in more detail later, but we have found small groups to be more effective places for people to experience authentic community. A home environment is certainly more warm and inviting than a sterile classroom setting. Since there are no time constraints, group meetings can occasionally run long without interfering with other programming. And since the size of the group is relatively small, this ensures that no one slips through the cracks. If a person doesn't show up, it is noticed.

Groups Offer Maximum Flexibility

In our small-group system, group members can schedule their own meeting times around their personal schedules. No one is tied down to meeting at one time on one particular day. The group can meet on the day they choose. Groups don't only offer flexibility *when* they meet, but also *where* they meet. They can meet anywhere or, if they so choose, they can rotate meeting locations.

Groups Allow Us to Be Better Stewards

Our groups strategy requires fewer church-owned and maintained facilities, which in turn frees up more money for other areas. If we were dependent on a Sunday morning class system, we would spend millions of dollars on space that stays empty most of the week. Our groups strategy allows us to be better stewards of what God has entrusted to us.

Groups Remove the Primary Limits to Growth

The main limits to growth for churches tend to be space and parking. When you are out of either, you have no choice but to build more. We will never run out of room or parking with our groups strategy, because people are meeting at homes in neighborhoods around the city. Our groups strategy has removed these primary limiting factors.

Many factors have contributed to our choosing the small-group model we use today. Our personal experience, as well as numerous strategic considerations, went into shaping our current approach. Other systems can work; we simply believe the small-group system is more effective. Effective in helping us accomplish our goal of leading people into a growing relationship with Jesus Christ. After all, that's what a strategy is for.

In the chapter to follow, we will discuss a unique characteristic of our small-group approach. In fact, this one distinctive has contributed more to the success of our strategy than perhaps anything. What is it? Come inside, close the door, and I'll fill you in.

CREATE YOUR COMMUNITY

1. What are the essentials of a great strategy?

2. What factors led your church to choose its strategy?

3. How does your strategy foster intentional relationships?

4. How does your strategy help people grow in their relationship with Christ?

5. What would be the advantages and disadvantages of small groups?

CHAPTER NINE

CLOSE THE DOOR

My office used to be located very close to our reception area. Being close to the front door had its advantages and its disadvantages. One advantage was that it allowed for quick transition times back to my office when I had an outside visitor. One disadvantage was that a lot of the foot traffic came right by my door. As a result, some well-meaning people felt very free to walk into my office unannounced. Regardless of what was going on, if the door was partially open, they viewed it as their invitation to come right in. So I regularly kept my door shut. I did not mean to be unfriendly; I just couldn't get much done with people coming in and out. I couldn't prioritize the people I already had appointments with or the work that I had to do when I was constantly interrupted.

So if I had a meeting, the door was closed. If I needed to focus on some work, the door was closed. If I wanted some time alone, the door was closed. If there was anything significant going on in my office—it happens occasionally—chances are, the door was shut. A closed door allowed me to concentrate and give my undivided attention to the people or project at hand. It allowed me to focus on the priorities and needs of the people I had already committed to. It allowed me to make the best use of their time and mine. Constant interruptions, distractions, or random drop-ins compromised the commitment and the attention I was able to give. As a result, people frequently heard me say, "Please close the door."

A distinctive of our small-group strategy is that we close the door. That is, we have *closed groups*. Purposefully so. We have given it a lot of thought, weighed the pros and cons, and have chosen to keep the participants in our groups as consistent as possible throughout an eighteen- to twenty-four-month covenant period. That is, unless a significant number of them drop dead or are raptured. If that happens, the dynamics of the group is the least of their problems!

By "closed groups," I mean that we encourage no new additions to the group unless the entire group signs off on it. Our rationale for having closed groups is simple. If disruptions work against the effectiveness of a meeting, then disruptions work against *any* meeting, small groups included. If interruptions compromise momentum by interfering with a person's focus, then interruptions will likewise compromise a small group—and the fulfillment of the group's promise.

PROMISES, PROMISES

Marketing experts will tell you that every company makes promises. Either directly or indirectly, every product or service promises to do something for the consumer. An organization's effectiveness is determined by how well it delivers on its promise.

Two years ago, we were introduced to a marketing company that came in to assess our small-group ministry. They helped us to gauge the awareness, participation, and experience of our regular attendees and members in our small groups. In essence, they measured how we were doing on the delivery of our promise. Our group promise is synonymous with the purpose statement for our community groups, which is "to provide a predictable small-group environment where participants experience authentic community and spiritual growth."

When I say we promise a "predictable" small-group experience, I know you may be laughing right about now. Small groups are anything but predictable, because they are filled with unpredictable people! After all, kids get sick, conflicts arise, crises occur. Life happens, and since life isn't predictable, how can groups be predictable?

When I say predictable, I'm talking about *who* the participants can expect to be attending their group. Our groups don't have revolving doors. The reason we are so protective is because we believe relationships take time to form. Anything that gets in the way of building the relational momentum of a group works against this reality. Every shared story, every common experience, every expressed dream or fear puts a plank in the relational platform of the group. In our opinion, open groups can become compromised by keeping them from experiencing the richness of community. When groups frequently change, they rip a plank right out of that relational foundation. And so we keep the doors closed for a season.

When I say predictable, I'm also referring to *what* participants can expect from their group. That's why our groups fill out covenants (see Appendix C to view North Point's covenant). We want the participants' expectations to be on the same page early as they begin their group experience. For example, we want them to be clear about the purpose for the group. Different people have had different group experiences and the assumed purpose for the group by one may be totally different for someone else. One person may be expecting a Bible study, another a support group, another a social gathering. Talk about a prescription for frustration!

We also want them to be clear about other aspects like the group's values (their standards for relating to each other) and guidelines (how frequently they will meet, where they will meet, and at what time). Many of these aspects are actually determined by the group itself. Groups that are constantly changing are forced to backtrack.

Open groups have a tendency to develop A.D.D. because they can become compromised in their outcome. As John Eldredge has written, "Small groups have become part of the programming that most churches offer their people. For the most part, they are short-lived." Eldredge goes on to say, "You can't just throw a random group of people together for a twelve-week study of some kind and expect them to become intimate allies."[28]

And, I would also add, you can't put a group of people together and constantly allow changes to their group, thereby interrupting their momentum, and expect them to become intimate allies.

A group that is not allowed to experience relational momentum becomes compromised and can lead to pseudo-community and a bad group experience. A bad group experience leads to an unfulfilled promise and dissatisfied group "customers." And dissatisfied group customers are a bad advertisement for your church, especially if it's the focus of your strategy.

Closed groups help a group member's experience to be as predictable as possible. They help the group produce the desired outcome, which for us is authentic community and spiritual growth.

AUTHENTIC COMMUNITY

At North Point, we define authentic community around the ABC's of group life—accountability, belonging, and care. Part of authentic community is *accountability*, which involves inviting other people into your life to challenge you in your priorities and relationships. These relationships obviously include your relationship with Christ, but also those with other believers and unbelievers.

A second part of authentic community is *belonging*. A person who has a sense of belonging is someone who feels accepted, connected, and comfortable with a group of people. This sense of connection is more important than ever because we live in a culture that is prioritizing belonging before believing. People need to know they matter and that they will be missed if they don't show up. People who are experiencing a sense of belonging are experiencing an important part of authentic community.

A third part of authentic community is *care*. A by-product of people connecting well is that they care for each other. People who are accountable to one another and are experiencing a sense of belonging naturally care for the people they are connected to. You don't have to program it. You don't have to force it. People care for people they know well.

People care for people they know well.

Jackie and Bob McGregor have experienced this reality first-hand. Last year, their son Doug was killed in an accident while riding his motorcycle. After getting word about the accident, they called one of the members of their community group and then headed to their daughter-in-law's house to be with her. Within minutes, couples from their community group were there providing Christ's comfort to these heartbroken parents. They would later say that without the support, love, and care of their group, they would not have made it. Care is a by-product of authentic community because you naturally care for people you know well.

Groups that constantly change seldom experience authentic community. They are weakened in their ability to deliver accountability, belonging, and care because they are never able to build the relational capital to get to that depth of relationship. In our opinion, closed groups allow people to more predictably experience authentic community.

SPIRITUAL GROWTH

Closed groups also allow us to better experience spiritual growth. Our desire is that when the group completes its two-year commitment, members can look back and see how God has used that time to encourage them, challenge them, and take them places in their relationship with God and others that they wouldn't have gone on their own.

As mentioned previously, we define spiritual growth around the continual pursuit of three vital relationships—intimacy with God, community with insiders, and influence with outsiders. Closed groups allow us to monitor a member's growth in these relationships over time. The group knows if members are struggling in their devotional life and how to provide ongoing encouragement. They have enough history together to provide it.

If a member has a challenging family relationship, the rest of the group has enough context and understanding to know how to best support them. A group that has history together knows each other's tendencies and how to keep one another moving in the right direction.

Finally, closed groups can better keep participants focused on the value of evangelism. Out of the three relationships, influence with outsiders tends to be the one that is naturally neglected. Yet nothing builds our faith more than when God uses us in the life of someone we have been trying to influence. And nothing changes the dynamic of a group more than when it has been praying for an unbeliever and sees that person connect with Christ.

CLOSED BUT FRESH

One legitimate concern of closed groups is that they become stagnant and inwardly focused over time. That's why our groups are closed only for a season. Our groups are challenged to multiply after their covenant period, usually in eighteen to twenty-four months. This keeps the group experience fresh and focused. When the group multiplies, it allows new people to bring what they most have to offer: new vitality to the group experience.

Granted, multiplication can be the most difficult aspect of group life. If you have a great group, the group will never want to multiply. If you have a marginal group, you won't be able to multiply fast enough! But like every living thing, every group has a life cycle. Every group eventually comes to an end. Our perspective is that a group can plan to end and have something to show for it, or they can let their group die a long, slow death.

Like every living thing, every group has a life cycle.

As Solomon reminds us in Ecclesiastes 3, for everything there is a season. And we believe for every group there is a season. And when that season is over, we open the door to let in fresh air and fresh relationships. And then we say again, "Please close the door," because there is still a lot to be done.

CREATE YOUR COMMUNITY

1. What is your organization's promise? How well does your organization deliver on its promise?

2. How important is predictability in establishing a strong relational foundation?

3. How would you define authentic community?

4. What are the advantages and disadvantages of open groups (where new people are always free to join)?

5. What are the advantages and disadvantages of closed groups?

Part

IV

CONNECTION
NEEDS
SIMPLICITY

CHAPTER TEN

CREATE STEPS

After graduating from college, I spent five years in sales management with the consumer goods company Procter & Gamble. One of the things that I came to appreciate while working for P&G was their marketing approach, or how they influenced consumers to purchase their brands.

It started with a commitment to manufacture the best products in each of the categories in which they competed. So P&G spent more money on research and development than any of their competitors. But as important as brand quality was, it all fell apart if consumers couldn't purchase the product at their local stores. If P&G did not successfully connect the retailer and customer with their product, then they could not make a sale and deliver the benefits of their quality products to consumers.

At North Point we have chosen a strategy centered on small groups because we believe it is the best delivery system for accomplishing our mission to lead people into a growing relationship with Jesus Christ. It is the best system for us to regularly encourage people to do what we want them to do, which is to pursue intimacy with God, community with insiders, and influence with outsiders. It reflects our belief about how people grow best—that is, in the context of structured and intentional relationships. And it best delivers on the way we have chosen to operate as a church—that is, relationally.

As important as small groups are in executing our strategy, it all falls apart if people have a difficult time connecting. If they cannot get into a group, then we cannot deliver on the benefits of a group. And then our strategy would be just another poorly executed idea.

One of the challenges to making connection simple in most churches is the fact that small groups are one of many options from which a person can choose. *Do I look for a class based on my age group? Do I look for a group in my neighborhood? Do I serve on a volunteer team? Do I assist with my child's activities? Do I do more than one thing?* Like stores in a mall, oftentimes there are too many options. That's why early on we adopted two practices that removed the fog from the connection process: We "clarified the win" and we began to "think steps, not programs."

CLARIFY THE WIN

Both of these practices are outlined more fully in *7 Practices of Effective Ministry*, but one of the first organizational decisions we made was to clarify our win. We determined what was really important to us and what really mattered. That's why early on we asked our three critical questions—*What do we want people to become? What do we want people to do?* and *Where do we want them to go?*—to help us clarify our wins. We determined one of our wins was for everyone to participate in a small group. Because of what God does in people's lives when they connect meaningfully, small-group involvement became an organizational win for us. We felt so strongly about it that the only numerical goal we have ever set as a church has been based on group participation.

THINKING STEPS

Clarifying the win not only made the end clearer, it also helped us to think about the steps that would be required to make the connection process work. That's why we implemented the practice to "think steps, not programs." As Reggie noted in *7 Practices*:

> Most churches are fairly effective at designing programs to meet needs. And the church staff usually feels like it is their responsibility to understand the needs of their

congregation and community and establish the appropriate programs to meet those needs. When you "think programs," your inclination tends to create something in order to meet specific needs that have surfaced in your attendee base or target group. When you "think steps" there is a fundamental difference in your perspective. Now the primary goal is not to meet someone's need but rather to help someone get where they need to go.

When you think *steps* you start by asking, "Where do we want people to be?" That question is followed by a second, more strategic question: "How are we going to get them there?" The result is a ministry that works as a step—it has been created to lead someone somewhere.[29]

As a result, we came up with three different "locations" to describe how our environments would connect people relationally and help move them into small groups. We call it our "Foyer to Kitchen" strategy. The following chart illustrates how it works. We believe church programs should not work in competition with each other, but work as steps to move people down a relational path to where we want them to go—into a small group. Like the rooms of a house, the environments of the church function for different purposes to help people connect.

THE FOYER

The foyer is the entry point of the home. Family and close friends don't enter through the foyer; it's primarily used by *guests*. When guests come to your home, you are sensitive to their needs and desires. You don't change what you believe as a family, but you are sensitive to the fact that they are there. For example, you don't discuss the family budget with guests. You also don't discuss the quirks of your neighbors. Certain things become irrelevant when you have guests in the house.

Our foyers at North Point are large environments designed to *change people's minds about church*. We have found that most people's problem today is not with God, but with the church. They view the church as being irrelevant to their everyday lives. As a result, they associate God with irrelevance. So it's our desire to make our foyers a place where people's minds are changed about church and, therefore, God as well. Our goal for this environment is for people to want to come back to church. They may not believe everything we believe when they leave, but we hope to have built enough of a bridge and created enough of a thirst that people will want to return.

Our foyers are large environments designed to change people's minds about church.

Our worship service is our best-known foyer environment because it tends to be the most utilized entrance by the unchurched. We have also designed foyers for most seasons of life, including families and students.

THE LIVING ROOM

The living room is designed for people to become better acquainted. The living room of a house is usually arranged in such a way that it allows people to casually connect. It is comfortable and inviting. The furniture is clustered to promote conversations. It is in the living room where guests begin to feel like *friends*.

Our living rooms are medium-sized environments designed to *change people's minds about connecting*. Our desire is that by the end of an evening, attendees will have made some connections with other people in their area of town and season of life. That's why we have built a "taste of community" into all of our living room environments. It might be a discussion group or a simple conversation with people at a table, but all of our living rooms are designed to help people connect and make new friends. Our hope is that people will want to take the next step into a small group after experiencing just a sample of group life. MarriedLife Live for couples and Fusion gatherings for singles are some of our better-known living room environments.

Our living rooms are medium-sized environments designed to change people's minds about connecting.

THE KITCHEN TABLE

The kitchen table is often where life's most meaningful conversations take place. It is here where people share their experiences, discuss important decisions, and enjoy meals. It's where people reveal their dreams and disclose their fears. The kitchen table is where close friends begin to feel more like *family*.

Our kitchen tables are our small-group environments. Our small groups have been designed to *change people's minds about their priorities*—that through the activity of God and the influence of their group, their priorities and God's priorities will line up; that over time, their lives will change.

Starting Point

We have two different kitchen table environments for adults. Starting Point is our starter track. It is a thirteen-week small-group environment that is targeted for seekers, starters, and returners. By *seekers*, we mean those who don't know Christ. Those who are admittedly outside the faith. Seekers who come to

Starting Point may come with a number of questions or simply attend at the invitation of a friend. By *starters*, we mean those who are new to the faith. These are brand-new Christians who are just starting out. We often say that these are the people who have just torn the cellophane off their Bibles. By *returners*, we mean those who are coming back to the church. Sometimes unsure where they fit on the spectrum of faith, they recognize that the response to life's challenges are not found away from Christ. These are the people who are blowing dust off their old Bibles.

Using a curriculum written by staff members Sean Seay, Lane Jones, Jason Malec, and several volunteer leaders, this is the place where people get answers to their really tough questions. Because of the target audience, it is one of our most exciting ministries. Many people have found or strengthened their faith through Starting Point.

Community Groups

Our other kitchen table environment and the primary small-group environment at North Point is a community group. Community groups are our growth track and consist of about six couples or eight individuals who covenant to meet for eighteen to twenty-four months. It is in this environment that we hope participants will pursue and experience authentic community (accountability, belonging, and care) and spiritual growth (intimacy with God, community with insiders, and influence with outsiders).

IT'S ALL ABOUT CHANGE

John is a great example of how God is using these group environments. He grew up in London with little spiritual influence. John moved to America in his twenties, doing the best he knew how, but he made several bad decisions and struggled through two failed marriages. Then God placed two influential people in his life. These two relationships made him aware of how much more life had to offer. He started attending North Point's worship service, then joined a Starting Point group, and then a community group. It was through his small-group experiences that he came to realize what it means to have a personal relationship with Jesus Christ day by day. John is a testimony to God's grace and the impact of a simple connection strategy.

Guests, friends, family. Foyer, living room, kitchen table. Each environment is designed to create a step. Each environment is designed to help people strategically connect. And each environment is designed to be a place God can use to change lives.

CREATE YOUR COMMUNITY

1. Do you have a connection strategy? If so, what is it?

2. Have you clarified the connection win for your organization?

3. Does your church think steps or programs? What are the advantages to thinking steps?

4. If small groups are one of many programming options at your church, how can you make them more aligned with your church's mission and strategy?

CHAPTER ELEVEN

MAKE THEM EASY

A few years ago, Andy walked into our general staff meeting with several sheets of construction paper. He took a blue sheet of paper and placed it on the floor at one end of the room and then took a green sheet and placed it on the floor thirty feet away. He then asked the staff, "If the blue paper represents groups and the green paper represents the worship service, then how are we going to get people to move from the green paper to the blue?" There was little response since we all thought it was a trick question. Knowing our propensity for playing jokes, a delayed response is usually wise.

Andy selected one of our staff members and asked her to

CREATING COMMUNITY

stand on the green piece of paper and, without touching the floor, step to the blue paper thirty feet away. The staff member looked at him in disbelief. She said, "I can't. It's too far away." He then put another sheet of paper on the floor alongside the green one, but no nearer the blue sheet, and asked her to try again using this new "step." Beginning to look frustrated, she said, "I still can't because the step is still too big." Andy quickly reminded her that he had provided another sheet of paper for her to use. She said, "But the new step is not helpful. The new step won't take me closer to where I need to go." And she was right. The new step was obvious, but it wasn't strategic. It didn't move her closer to the goal. It was merely "sideways energy"—it didn't help her get where she wanted to go.

Andy used this simple illustration to teach us that for a step to be effective, it needs to be *easy*, *obvious*, and *strategic*. If the step is not *easy*, people won't be able to take it. Or if they try, they will usually fail. If the step is not *obvious*, if people can't see how the step will take them where they want to go, they may not even try. If the step is not *strategic*, then the step will not take them where they need to go. The scenery might be nice, but it won't take people to the desired destination.

For a step to be effective, it needs to be easy, obvious, and strategic.

ADDING A STEP

Our original living room "step" for married couples was the area fellowship. These gatherings were medium-sized environments designed to help people connect relationally and move into small groups. These monthly gatherings occurred in homes according to season of life and geographic area and were effective in bringing people together. Occasionally.

Due to varying schedules and kids' activities, attendance at these gatherings for most people was inconsistent, which made the gatherings ineffective at connecting people to groups. If you missed one month, it might be two or three months before you saw the same faces again. And so area fellowships were not an easy step for connecting couples into group life.

Under the effective leadership of Rebekah Lyons, the director of our married area fellowships, her team created the idea for an additional step. Rather than hold onto the area fellowship concept as the primary way to connect couples, she and her team created a step, an event that would help connect people quickly into small groups. We call it GroupLink.

GROUPLINK

GroupLink is a two-hour event where people connect with others in their geographic area and stage of life to start a community group. GroupLink usually takes place four times a year, in January, March, August, and October, the months we have found to be peak connection times for groups. Leading up to each GroupLink, our service programming team builds awareness in our worship services through bulletin inserts, videos, and announcements. Additionally, Andy preaches at least one message on community each year, usually before a scheduled GroupLink. Getting people connected into a group is truly a team effort!

It's All About the Environment

Mitzi Miller and her outstanding assimilation team have truly perfected the GroupLink process. The GroupLink experience begins the moment a person arrives. There is a check-in team waiting to welcome the attendees and provide them with name tags. The attendees then walk into an inviting environment designed for their stage of life. The room has been decorated, music is playing, and generous hors d'oeuvres platters await them. People are then directed to their designated tables with other people from their area of town. Once attendees have had time to eat and break the ice, a staff host welcomes everyone and reminds them of the goal of the evening—to bring people together who want to connect and help them form a group.

It's Caught on Tape

Recognizing that people come into the night with differing expectations, we present a helpful ten-minute video to clarify what they can realistically expect from a group. Using a humorous sketch and personal testimonies, the video creatively communicates to the attendees what a community group is and is not. It shows that it's not a social club, a meditation group, a support group, or even a teacher-driven group; rather, it's a group that meets weekly in a home for fellowship, Bible study, and prayer. Then several people share their stories about how God has used their groups to change their lives. This video can be viewed in its entirety by going to www.grouplinkvideo.org.

Time to Go Fish

Then group leaders are introduced by name, group location, and the day they can meet. Often attendees have already formed their new groups with the people sitting around them. If not, attendees join the leader whose meeting time and location best suits their needs. Once a group is full, the leader collects the new group's information (names, phone numbers, and e-mail addresses) and they agree on a start date. Most connected groups start within two weeks of the GroupLink. Attendees are then dismissed to get more food or to talk further with the people who now make up their new group.

CONNECTION MADE EASY

As the accompanying chart illustrates, North Point's connection strategy is very simple. There are only three ways attendees can connect into a community group. They can (1) connect through the relationships they make in a living room environment; (2) through the relationships they make while attending Starting Point; or (3) through GroupLink. Of all three, GroupLink is now the primary way we connect people into group life. That's it. It's that simple. When I look at some group-connection strategies, I am convinced that electrical engineers designed them. There are so many boxes, so many lines, so many options, and so much complexity, it's no wonder people have a tough time knowing what to do or where to go!

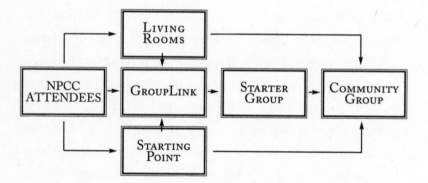

Here's the exciting part. GroupLink is now enabling us to connect *90 percent* of the people who attend this event into a group. We are on target to connect over three thousand people into small groups this year alone! Only God knows what this will mean in the long run, but it makes me think of the struggling marriages that will potentially be saved. I think of the discouraged single person who will be encouraged to wait for God's best. I think of the successful businessperson who will begin to invest his life in kingdom purposes. All because they are well connected with men and women just like themselves who want to grow in their relationship with Christ. And all because the process to connect them was simple to understand and do.

The experience of Stephen and Jana has been repeated many times over at GroupLink:

We were encouraged by a friend to attend North Point. After visiting for just six weeks, we jumped into the NPCC experience. We never saw the same faces during Sunday services, but that was okay—we had plenty of friends and didn't really need any more. Then one Sunday morning, Andy echoed those same exact thoughts. He went on to speak about community groups and something called a GroupLink. We decided to take one more step of commitment at North Point by signing up that Sunday.

Andy had mentioned that the emotions of attending GroupLink were similar to a dating experience, and he was right! We were sure no one there would live near us. The Attic (our student ministry room) was filled with other couples in their thirties and forties, none of whom we knew. When we were told to stand up and mingle, we stood up, turned around, and started talking to the three couples beside us. Two more couples walked over, and before we knew it, God had formed a community group with other people in our area without us even taking a step. We went home that Saturday night feeling slightly amazed. It was all so easy.

What about your connection process? Is it helping you to realize your small-groups potential? Is it helping you to connect the unconnected? GroupLink is certainly not the only way to connect people into groups, but it has been effective for us. The process is *easy* (sign-ups come through the bulletin or on-line), it's *obvious* (GroupLink is *the* step for people wanting to get into a group), and it's *strategic* (it takes people where we want them to go). It has proven to be helpful for connecting people into small groups.

But that raises a question. What do you do if after five weeks you find you don't really enjoy the people you have been connected with? Once the group forms, what happens if the group doesn't gel? Are you stuck? Should you fake a serious illness? Do you just hang in there for eighteen months? What do you do?

CREATE YOUR COMMUNITY

1. What are the steps to community in your church?

2. Are the steps easy? How could they be made easier?

3. Are the steps obvious? How could they be made more obvious?

4. Are the steps strategic? How can they do a better job of taking people in the right direction?

5. Do you have too many steps? Do you have too few?

CHAPTER TWELVE

TRY BEFORE
YOU BUY

Automobile dealers are getting smarter. They know that one of the reasons people are hesitant to buy or lease a car is fear. With so many options today, consumers dread making a wrong decision. They fear contracting the near-fatal sickness known as "buyer's remorse." Skittish consumers are phobic about making a purchase and then finding out they could have gotten a cheaper deal or purchased a better model. But now, having made the purchase, they are trapped. There's no way out. They're stuck with their purchase. At least for the life of the loan or lease. Chances are, you have suffered from this ailment. Most of us have. The result? You become indecisive in your buying. You

begin to second-guess yourself. You are more hesitant to make the next purchase.

So some automobile manufacturers have begun to allow potential buyers to take their cars home and test them. It's the "try before you buy" concept. Try it, and if you like it, you keep it. If you don't, you return it, no questions asked. It gives the shopper time to become familiar with the car, to make sure it's the right set of wheels for them. If they don't like the vehicle or find something better, they don't have to keep it. Most of the time, however, consumers end up keeping the car. That's why manufacturers make the offer: It's a smart move.

THE EIGHT-WEEK DATE

One of the barriers to a person's joining a small group can be this same decision-making phobia. Some people fear they will be trapped if they join a group—that after a few weeks, the group will not be what they wanted or expected and *it will be too late*. They'll be stuck. And so for the next eighteen to twenty-four months, they will be condemned to group hell. So they don't bother to join. They remain in isolation. And they miss out on all the benefits a small group can bring.

A starter group is a group that 'dates' for eight weeks.

This is where GroupLink is unique. We do not ask people to commit themselves to a long-term group with people they don't know. We believe that's unreasonable. Rather, participants come out of GroupLink having joined a *starter group*, which is a group that "dates" for eight weeks. If the group gels, they continue on for the entire covenant period as a fully functioning community group. If it doesn't, no hard feelings. No questions asked. They simply go to the next GroupLink and try again. But this usually is not necessary. Over 90 percent of the groups connected at GroupLink continue on after the eight-week starter period. God does a great job of putting people together. And we give them an "out" that provides them peace of mind throughout the process.

We also take several steps to set our starter groups up for success.

Staff Coach

Each starter group leader is assigned to a staff person for the eight-week period. The role of the staff member is to monitor the group's progress and to shepherd the leader through the starter period. We ask our staff to connect at least twice with each of their starter group leaders during this "dating" time.

New Group DVD

We also provide each new group with a DVD that we request they show during their first group meeting. The DVD revisits the purpose and priorities of a North Point community group and discusses some of the things they can do to get the most out of their group experience. It reminds them of what they can expect from the group and what their group is expecting from them— namely, their active and consistent participation. We believe setting clear expectations from the beginning is part of the prescription for a successful group.

Setting clear expectations from the beginning is part of the prescription for a successful group.

Leader Guide and Curriculum

We provide each leader with a leader's guide for the starter group. The guide is divided into four sections. The first section is a guide to facilitating a group, addressing issues like meeting frequency and prioritizing the relationships of the group over the curriculum. The second section provides an overview and some pointers for using their starter curriculum. We provide all participants with a curriculum for the starter period because we want to make sure everyone begins well. The third section provides weekly objectives for all eight sessions. There is a stated objective for the evening, a suggested icebreaker, and leader notes focused on the central ideas for that night's discussion.

The last section is critically important. It is the "next steps" section and guides the leaders through the appropriate next steps after the starter period has concluded. It provides them with a few suggestions for their next curriculum, informs them of future training opportunities, and reminds the group leaders to fill out a covenant.

Try before you buy. It is a concept that is working well for many industries. And it is working well for the community group ministry at North Point. It provides peace of mind for the participants and sets a group up for success.

SIMPLE IS BETTER

This is all part of a simple connection strategy. Because connection needs simplicity. If people cannot get into a group, then we cannot deliver on the benefits of a group. We responded to this issue by coming up with different categories to describe how our ministry environments would connect people and ultimately move them into group life. And when our steps weren't easy enough, we added a new one called GroupLink with a "try before you buy" guarantee. It's a lot of effort, but the alternative—disconnected, isolated, lonely people—is not a viable option. We feel that only connected people can be fully led into a growing relationship with Christ. Only connected people can be encouraged to pursue intimacy with God, community with insiders, and influence with outsiders. And only connected people change over the long haul. And that's what it is all about.

CREATE YOUR COMMUNITY

1. What are some barriers for people getting into a small group?

2. Have you experienced the fear of being trapped in a bad group? Would a "try before you buy" option have relieved your fears?

3. Why is establishing clear expectations from the beginning so important for a group's success? How could you do this effectively in your setting?

4. What tools do you provide a new group leader? Are there any additional items that would better position them for success?

Part
V

PROCESSES
NEED
REALITY

DEAL IN REALITY

Turn on primetime television these days and chances are you'll land on a reality show. The rash of these shows can be attributed to a number of factors, but one thing is for sure: They are here to stay. Viewers are voting to see real people deal with real issues in the real world. We are tired of poorly written sitcoms with scripted endings. So we're tuning in by the millions to reality TV.

For groups to work, the systems we design also need to be based in reality. Our expectations need to be reasonable, and our processes must be made for people who live in the real world. Otherwise, the very systems created to implement our groups will be nothing more than unrealistic scripts.

LIVING IN THE REAL WORLD

Not long ago, a humorous airlines commercial aired featuring a salesman at his desk answering phone calls from prospective clients. They all wanted to meet with him—a salesman's dream. But there was one problem. They all wanted to meet with him the same week and they were all in different cities. "Memphis on Tuesday? I can do that. Dallas on Wednesday? I can do that. Little Rock on Thursday? I can do that. Detroit on Friday? I can do that." After his last call, he hangs up the phone and says, "Now how am I going to do that?" The salesman knew it was impossible for him to do what he had just promised. As much as he wanted to do it all, when he made these commitments he wasn't dealing in reality.

We found ourselves in a similar situation a few years ago with our groups system. We use a version of the Meta model, which includes three levels of leadership: the group leader (a volunteer), the coach (a volunteer), and the division leader (a staff member). Now the coach is responsible for shepherding five to seven group leaders. If you looked at our position description for the coach, the expectations were clear: We were *only* asking coaches to gather with their leaders in a huddle three times a year. We were *only* asking them to meet one-on-one with their leaders six times a year. We were *only* asking them to attend four training events a year. We were *only* asking them to participate in one GroupLink a year. Our expectations for our coaches were very clear, that much is certain. That wasn't the problem.

In a strategy development meeting one of our staff members, Al Scott, mentioned that his coaches were frustrated. When asked why, he said it was because we were asking them to do too much. In his opinion, our expectations were unrealistic. The team's initial response was to push back. But when we stopped to think about it, Al was right. I was a coach myself and I wasn't able to keep up with all we were asking to be done! When all our expectations were tallied up, we were asking the average coach to lead or attend *forty* things a year. Additionally, we wanted him to participate in a group. Experience had taught us that the average volunteer has time to do no more than twenty things a year, and we were asking our coaches to do *twice* that much. No wonder they were frustrated! We had set our coaches up for failure. So we reduced their workload by 60 percent and involved them in only the things that were absolutely essential.

Group processes have to work with the average person in mind.

If our groups are going to be effective, the processes we put in place have to be realistic. They have to be able to work with the average person in mind. People want to make a difference, but they also have other important responsibilities. Priorities like family, friends, and jobs. Are your leadership processes realistic? It's a good question to ask yourself.

REASONABLE QUALIFICATIONS

Another question to ask yourself is how reasonable are your criteria for choosing leaders? I am all for qualified people serving as point leaders for our small groups, but when I look at the standards that have been established in some churches, it appears that formal sainthood must be conferred upon a person before they can lead. Qualifications are meant to keep *some* people out of leadership, not *all* people out of leadership!

We make a distinction between a person who leads a *group meeting* and a person who leads a *group*. A person who leads a group meeting can be anyone in the group who is comfortable with navigating the discussion. The value of broader involvement is so great, we think it offsets any risk involved. After all, what's the worst thing that can happen with an approved point leader present? But the potential benefit after a person has spent time preparing and interacting with biblical truth can be profound. Because of this, we encourage our groups to rotate responsibility for leading the discussion.

Qualifications are meant to keep some people out of leadership, not all people out of leadership.

A person who leads or oversees a group, on the other hand, is someone we expect to meet five reasonable criteria.

First, leaders have to be *connected.* They must be members of North Point. Membership communicates to us that a person is a Christ follower and wants to formally partner with us in our mission to lead people into a growing relationship with Jesus Christ.

Second, they need to have *character.* They need to be known by others as people of integrity and solid reputation.

Third, leaders must embrace our groups *culture.* By that, we mean that they support and subscribe to our small-group strategy and values, including apprenticing and multiplication.

Fourth, they must have good *chemistry* with staff and other leaders. They need to be team players and the type of people others benefit from being around.

Fifth, leaders need to have a level of *competence.* When it comes to overseeing a group, whether in a previous leadership role or as an apprentice, they need to have demonstrated the passion and skills to serve as point leader of a group.

The first criterion is established through membership. The other four are determined through a leader application and an interview with a staff member.

REALISTIC EXPECTATIONS

Not only do our leader qualifications need to be reasonable, so do our expectations. If qualifications clarify *who* should lead, then expectations clarify *what* the leader does when they lead. When leader expectations become unrealistic or unclear, as with our coaches, then the effectiveness of the group is compromised.

The role of the leader is simply to serve as a shepherd in two ways: by facilitating the group and by monitoring the group.

By *facilitating* the group, we mean facilitating the organization of the group. This has to do more with process issues, such as the logistics of the group, where the group is headed, when and where the group meets, who is leading the group, and what the group will be studying.

By *monitoring* the group, we mean checking the pulse or health of the group. This has to do more with people issues, such as how connected people are feeling, how openly people are sharing, how much people are growing, and whether the group is poised to multiply (see Appendix B for a complete Groups Leader description).

WILLING TO CHANGE

We began this chapter by saying that for groups to work, the processes that define them must work. They must be realistic. They can't just look good on paper. Which implies there will be occasions when parts of the system have to be more carefully scrutinized. At times the system may require a major overhaul. We recently experienced this ourselves.

As I shared, our groups process has been dependent upon volunteer coaches to lead our leaders. Outside of two major training events a year, the role of the coach has been to shepherd and develop five leaders. When we recognized that our expectations for our coaches were unrealistic, we fixed this glitch. But after we did, we realized there was even a greater crack in the foundation. We had to dig deeper.

We had assumed that it was reasonable to expect a volunteer coach to consistently develop their group leaders. We discovered it is not. We found that it was reasonable for a coach to monitor their groups, but not develop their group leaders, and there is a big difference. When I talk to friends around the country in positions like mine, I consistently hear that the coaching process is their biggest challenge and the Achilles' heel of every groups system of any size. Every one. So we have changed the way we coach leaders by removing the "middle man" and giving the coaching responsibility directly to our staff group directors. (The Meta model refers to them as division leaders.)

Rather than shepherd seventy-five leaders through fifteen coaches, the only responsibility of our groups directors (staff people) is to shepherd sixty leaders (see Appendix A for a complete Director position description). We are very excited about this modification in leader coaching. And so are our former coaches. We all are confident this change will allow us to improve in the area of leader development and give our directors more hands-on influence over the success and effectiveness of their groups. Though we expect this fine-tuning of our model to be a vast improvement, it won't be our last change. As the saying goes, when you are through changing, you are through.

Reasonable qualifications, realistic expectations, and occasional modifications. All three contribute to a groups system that deals in reality.

CREATE YOUR COMMUNITY

1. What are your criteria for choosing leaders? Are they reasonable?

2. What are the advantages and disadvantages to allowing group members to rotate group meeting leadership?

3. What kinds of expectations do you have for group leaders? Are they clear? Are they reasonable?

4. What are the strengths and weaknesses of your leadership structure? Do any changes need to be made?

CHAPTER FOURTEEN

TRAIN LESS FOR MORE

I have attended my fair share of "how-to" conferences and seminars. They have covered topics like how to live, how to pray, how to grow, how to share, how to counsel, how to communicate, how to be married, how to deal with conflict (are these mutually exclusive?), how to spend time with God, how to raise kids, how to lead a small group, how to lead a team, how to work with different personalities, and on and on.

Most of these conferences have been long and provided more information than I ever could apply. However, each did provide me with my very own notebook. Inside these costly binders are the notes I took from each of the numerous sessions

I attended. These notes include lists of the things I was now sup-posed to implement into my already overloaded life. For years, my post-conference routine was predictable. I would grab my newly acquired notebook, put it in a cabinet, look at it one last time, and then, with a tinge of guilt, close the door and go on with life. Suffering from information overload, I did what any overwhelmed person would do: I removed the notebook from my sight and the guilt that came with it. Ever been there?

A few years ago, a friend of mine challenged me to manage my learning process a little more effectively by writing down the main takeaways when I am exposed to new information. It could be from a conference or my time with God. It could be from a sermon or a weeklong event. It could be from a one-hour meet-ing or a weekend retreat. The process was the same. I would summarize the information in a few takeaway points. I would distill the lessons to their most important elements. This process has been helpful as I try to move from being an *acquirer* of infor-mation to an *applier* of information.

MORE OR LESS?

Again, for groups to work, the systems that define them must work. That means they must be realistic. They must be designed for real people who live in the real world.

For example, most leader training seemingly embraces the "more is more" approach. This view suggests that effective training is about exposing people to a lot of information—the more the better. The assumption is that the more information leaders are exposed to, the better prepared they will be to lead. But, like the conference notebook gathering dust on the shelf, it is not the acquisition of information that properly prepares a leader to lead; rather, it is the application of the *right information*. People need to be trained around the core principles they need to know, not an endless amount of information that is nice for them to know.

The "train less for more" ideal is derived from the "teach less for more" practice outlined in *7 Practices of Effective Ministry*. This principle states that you can actually improve how much people learn if you teach them less:

> The things you choose to teach should be limited to those things that your people most need to hear—in other words, the core principles most appropriate to your target audience. These are what we refer to as the "irreducible minimums" of learning.
>
> If you are responsible for training in your organization, you must learn to prioritize information. You have to look at what your target audience needs to know and separate what is most important from what is just interesting. Why? Because you have a limited amount of time to communicate with these people. And when it comes to information, all knowledge is not equal. There are

facts that are nice to know, and then there is information that is really interesting. But much more important, there is a body of knowledge that is critical for certain individuals in your organization to understand. Good teachers first identify what is critical for others to know.[30]

To "train less for more" means that we narrow the scope of what we train our leaders on, so we can say more about the things that matter most. This process begins by identifying what leaders really need to know in order to be effective in their roles. Not everything we *wish* they could know, but the irreducible minimums they *need* to know. Because some things are more important for leaders to know and do than others.

Some things are more important for leaders to know and do than others.

OUR ESSENTIALS

Some time ago, we came up with our own irreducible minimums for our community group leaders. We believe these six essentials are critical to leading well. If our leaders will implement these six priorities, we feel they will be extremely effective in leading their groups.

Think Life-Change

Bill Hybels has said that vision leaks. And that is definitely true when it comes to the vision and purpose for groups. It is easy for groups to drift away from their main purpose. So this value reminds our leaders why we have groups: to create a predictable environment where participants experience authentic community and spiritual growth. An environment where God is active in the lives of its members. A small group where people *change*. Keeping the life-change goal in front of leaders challenges them to keep their groups purposeful.

Cultivate Relationships

This essential focuses on how leaders build a sense of community in their groups. We remind them that relationships are like bank accounts: They don't just happen. They require regular intentional deposits. Starting early to build the relational capital of the group is one of the most important steps leaders can take. We encourage leaders to plan activities such as an overnight in the first six months of their time together as groups. We suggest that they then make ongoing deposits to continually cultivate relationship among the group members. Some examples are:

- Volunteer on a ministry team or for a service project together.
- Rotate names and go out with another group member or couple every other month.

- Have a family get-together (e.g., pool party, cookout, camping trip).
- Participate on a short-term mission project together.
- For couples groups, have the men and women split up during prayer time.

Planned deposits bring greater relational satisfaction to a group's balance sheet.

Relationships are like bank accounts: They require regular, intentional deposits.

Promote Participation

One of our more encouraging group experiences happened when a quieter member led for the first time. It was exciting to see him come prepared and share in a way we had not seen up to that point. His leading gave him confidence for greater participation in the future.

This essential focuses on how the leader leads the group meeting. It reminds leaders that since shared participation creates broader ownership of the group, all group members should be encouraged to participate often in the facilitation and leadership of the group meeting.

This essential also reminds leaders to promote participation by being navigators of discussion, not teachers of curriculum. The difference is critical. Every time leaders ask open-ended questions, they are inviting participation. More than sharing the right answers, we want people to share their lives.

More than sharing the right answers, we want people to share their lives.

Replace Yourself

This essential encourages leaders to intentionally apprentice someone in their group for future leadership. The apprentice is someone who has the potential to replace a leader, not simply assist him. Since adults often learn on a need-to-know basis, we have discovered that apprenticing is the most effective way to identify and train group leaders. When you put someone into the game, he or she learns quickly. We encourage leaders to identify an apprentice within the first six months of the group. This assures that the group is fully prepared to multiply at the end of the covenant period.

Provide Care

While working on this manuscript, the wife of one of our group leaders was tragically killed in an automobile accident. I received nine calls in less than forty minutes. While I was frustrated to not be in town at the time of the accident, I knew that the members of this man's community would rally around him. And they did. Those from current and past groups were at his side. Multiple staff members were also with him. His kids' group leaders were with his two sons. Jesus' hands and feet sprang into action to walk with this grieving family during a terrible time. That's because people instinctively care for those with whom they have a relationship. I received the following e-mail from this man the day after his wife's funeral:

> Andy likes to call North Point "the world's most generous church." Can we add "most caring church"?

This essential reminds leaders that the primary way we provide care to our attendees is through community groups. It equips the leaders on how to deal with challenging situations in their groups. It also informs them of the additional care ministry resources available from the church.

Multiply Influence

This final essential reminds leaders that multiplying their groups opens the door for others to participate in group life. It also allows them the opportunity to multiply their influence. While we recognize this to be the most difficult aspect of group leadership, it can also be the most rewarding.

As the following chart indicates, if people simply multiply their groups every eighteen months, they will have impacted almost two hundred people in six years. Another four years and they begin to experience the power of exponential growth. In a little over ten years, one leader will have personally influenced more than fifteen hundred people! Group multiplication allows leaders to impact more lives than they could any other way.

Year	# of People
Today	12
1.5	24
3	48
4.5	96
6	192
7.5	384
9.0	768
10.5	1536

PLAY IT AGAIN

Once we identified these six essentials, we began to use them. Over and over again. In fact, they are the basis for all of our training events. In our orientation for new leaders, we provide an overview of each one. We review them during one-on-one meetings between group directors and their leaders. At both of our annual training events, we take one essential and drill down designing an entire event around it. This allows leaders to be trained on all six essentials every three years.

Training less for more is the way to go. While leaders need training on some things, what they need most is training on the important things. Narrowing the scope of training to the irreducible minimums, then saying them over and over again, gives leaders the essentials they need. Essentials to lead effective, life-changing groups.

CREATE YOUR COMMUNITY

1. What kind of leadership training do you provide?

2. What should be the irreducible minimums for your leaders?

3. Do you tend to teach "more for more" or "less for more"?

4. What are some advantages of the "train less for more" approach?

5. How can you "train less for more" in your setting?

CHAPTER FIFTEEN

SET UP FOR SUCCESS

Being a church of small groups was our goal from the start. However, in the first two years, North Point chose to focus its attention on creating relevant foyer and living room environments. With limited staff, investing into these areas needed to be the priority in order to attract the most unchurched people. We knew we needed to attract people before we could connect people. So we started there. Unfortunately, it prevented us from fully developing our small groups ministry. Our groups were being loosely directed by several of us, and we did not have a designated point leader.

Thankfully, a lot has changed. Over the past seven years, our small groups organization has received the focus needed to set it up to win. If groups are going to succeed, they must be set up well. I believe there are five factors that position a small groups ministry for success.

SIMPLE

One factor is to keep your church's strategy simple. We don't try to do everything. Instead, we try to do a few things well. This allows us to focus on moving people through our foyer and living room environments into small groups. At North Point, if a ministry isn't a step toward community, we don't do it. And we have created one primary path into community, GroupLink, which makes connection easy. A simple strategy allows us to do less while accomplishing more.

If a ministry isn't a step toward community, we don't do it.

I can't overstate this point. Simple systems are easier to understand, easier to communicate, and easier to implement. Simple is simply better.

VISIBLE

Visibility sets a group system up for success. The more visible groups are, the more people get the message that they are important and a priority for our church. We have been able to keep our groups visible in several ways.

First, Andy speaks on community often. Having the senior leader devote messages to the subject of small groups speaks volumes to our attendees.

Second, we promote GroupLink five times a year in our worship services. Taking time to communicate the process and importance of connection keeps groups front and center.

Third, the way we do baptism also allows our attendees to regularly hear about the value of groups. I believe our approach is truly one of North Point's best practices. Before people are baptized, we require them to record a brief video testimony. It is a great opportunity for those being baptized to publicly thank all who have played a role in their faith journey. It is also incredible advertising for small groups. The majority of those baptized conclude by thanking the members of their small group for their influence and encouragement. Obviously, this sends a huge message: that small groups are a vehicle God uses to change lives. The best advertisement is always a satisfied customer whose life has been changed.

VALUED

Another factor that sets up a group system for success is that it is valued. And what's valued is what's celebrated. Since group life is how we "do church," it is constantly celebrated through our announcements, sketches, and sermon illustrations. It is part of the DNA of North Point.

A defining moment came for us several years ago after our leadership team worked through Jim Collins's *Built to Last*. This outstanding book is about the successful habits of visionary companies. We had just read the chapter on how visionary companies used BHAGs (Big Hairy Audacious Goals) as tools to stimulate progress, so we discussed what our BHAG should be. We knew we didn't want it to be based on Sunday attendance, because that would only tell part of the story. We knew we didn't want the BHAG to be financial, because that wouldn't gauge life change. The team agreed that our goals should be centered around group participation.

So we prayed and leveraged our efforts as an organization to reach the goal of moving seventy-two hundred adults into groups within five years. That may not seem like a big goal for a church our size, but we had only eight hundred and fifty adults in groups at the time. We all smiled when we set the goal because it seemed so unrealistic. Because of God's activity and the concentrated efforts of our entire team, we reached this challenging goal in just four years.

That one goal, that one decision, communicated more about

the value of groups to our leaders than anything else we could have done.

RESOURCED

You can tell a lot about a person by how he spends his money. You can tell a lot about churches the same way. They invest in what they value. Without the appropriate resources, no groups system will ever get off the ground.

> **Without the appropriate resources, no groups system will ever get off the ground.**

Investing resources in three areas paid off significantly for us. The first area was *personnel*. When we committed to provide specialized staff in areas like assimilation and leader development, we saw immediate results. We gave focused attention to developing our GroupLink processes and to our leader-training initiatives. As a result, we were able to assimilate large numbers of people in a relatively short period of time. Providing adequate staff support has been key.

The second area that we committed resources to was *training*. We concentrate most of our training around three events, which have been adequately funded to make these times relevant and creative. There is consistency in what our leaders experience on Sundays and what they experience at one of our training events. Our goal is to do both with excellence, and, as a result, participation is high.

The third area that we committed resources to was *childcare*. We determined early on that childcare issues could be a potential barrier for people, so we had a couple of options. We could ignore the issue, which would reduce participation, or we could build adult classrooms, which would cost millions. Neither of these options appealed to us. So we came up with a third possibility. We chose to reimburse people at a predetermined rate for their childcare expenses (see Appendix E for an explanation of our childcare reimbursement policy). We invest a pretty good sum of money every year on childcare, but it's less than paying debt service on buildings that would sit empty for most of the week.

MODELED

I am grateful that we have a senior leader who views small-group participation as a personal passion and not just a program. And so is our church. Andy's personal involvement and leadership has contributed significantly to the success of our groups ministry. It has allowed him to speak passionately about the value of groups and to speak honestly about how God has used them in his life.

SET UP FOR SUCCESS

He has led a small group from the beginning and has consistently modeled the way for us as a church. As in any church, the senior leader is the real point leader for groups, and it is no different at North Point.

You cannot put enough value on seeing key leadership participate in group life. It sends just one more reminder of the importance of small groups to the strategy and health of the church. Without the participation of senior leadership, a point leader is in the unenviable position of marketing a ministry that key leadership doesn't fully support.

You cannot put enough value on seeing key leadership participate in group life.

There are many things that can set up a groups system for success. For us, what's most important is making the strategy simple, keeping the message visible, valuing the processes, providing adequate resources, and modeling participation. Each contributes to create a process that looks good on paper and works well in reality.

After all, processes need reality. They need to be shaped by what works. So our leader expectations need to be reasonable. Our shepherding systems need to be effective, and our training processes need to train leaders on what's essential. Our group systems need to be set up for success. Otherwise, the very systems created to deliver effective groups will be compromised. They will be nothing more than unrealistic scripts. And when we consider what's at stake—people's lives—that option is unacceptable.

CREATE YOUR COMMUNITY

1. What factors do you believe make for a successful ministry strategy?

2. Would you describe your strategy as simple or complex?

3. We have identified five factors that set up a ministry for success. In your opinion, are all five important? Why or why not?

4. Which are present in your current strategy? Which are absent?

5. In your opinion, what needs to occur to better position your ministry for success?

A FINAL THOUGHT

We wrote *Creating Community* because we believe very passionately that people need to experience community life, and because we have seen what happens when people don't. The material we have shared has been instrumental in creating a thriving small-groups culture at North Point.

After reading a book like this, it is natural to ask, "What now?" We aren't so arrogant as to suggest that you jettison what you are currently doing, but we do hope you will take the time to ask yourself some hard questions in the five key areas we have shared. We suggest you pick one or two of them, the ones your organization is most hungry for, then discuss them as a team.

For example, we hope you will talk about people's very real need for community. Starbucks is a great place to get a cup of coffee, but it doesn't offer the One who can change people's lives. Now, more than ever, people need what only the church can provide: authentic, biblical community. Everyone—you, me, our families, our neighbors, our coworkers—all of us have a built-in need to connect meaningfully with a few people. "In community" is how God intended us to experience life. It is how He has hardwired our souls. While people don't need more things to attend, they do need the kind of life-giving benefits that occur when people connect regularly in a meaningful way. Larry Crabb says it well: "As our lungs require air, so our souls require what only community provides. We were designed…to live in relationship. Without it we die. It's that simple."[31]

Or you may need to evaluate the clarity of your church's mission and how you hope to accomplish it. I believe the three critical questions we struggled with—*What do we want people to become? What do we want people to do?* and *Where do we want people to go?*—can serve as a good starting point. Ask your team members how they would respond to these questions. If their answers are different, chances are your leaders need clarity.

Or you may need to scrutinize your ministry strategy and how it is helping you (or not helping you) achieve your mission. While churches need strategies that are clear and compelling, most of all they need strategies that work. They need strategies that will produce the desired outcomes and help fulfill the organization's promise. This may entail a minor tweak to a program, the elimination of a competing program, or a major overhaul of the whole system. But an honest discussion of your strategy's effectiveness and shortcomings can only help you and your organization in the future.

Or you may need to inspect your connection strategy and determine how easy it is for the average participant to join a small group. People will never come to experience the benefits of your ministry unless they can easily connect into it. Have you created a maze or steps to connection? If you have provided steps, are they easy, obvious, and strategic?

Finally, you may need to evaluate your processes and consider just how feasible they are for the average user. For example, we hope you will reassess the expectations you have for your volunteers and make adjustments where needed. Our processes either serve our leaders and volunteers or they are forced to become subservient to our processes. That's why our processes need to be reasonable, designed for people in the real world.

A word of caution. Pace yourself when it comes to making changes. Too much change too fast is unhealthy for any established organization. While I have discussed in detail some of the principles and strategies we use at North Point, they are only meant to stimulate your thinking and cause you to ask some important questions. Bottom line, these strategies work for us. And we think they can work in a lot of places. But remember, every church is unique. Before making any changes or adding new strategies, be sure to consider your church's culture, leadership, and programming philosophies.

God has a dream for us, and I believe it includes authentic community. Jesus prayed for it. It's what we all need and what the unbelieving world longs to see. I take great comfort in the fact that community is God's idea. That means He will assume ultimate responsibility for making His dream come true. Our prayer is that what you have read here will help make His dream your reality. And a reality for many others as well.

GROUPS DIRECTOR POSITION DESCRIPTION

Purpose

A Community Groups Director at North Point Community Church is responsible for shepherding and leading sixty to seventy-five group leaders by encouraging and equipping them to personally pursue the three vital relationships and to create a predictable small-group environment around the six leader essentials.

Profile

The profile of a Community Groups Director should be a blend between people and task personality traits. He/she also should have one or more of the following spiritual gifts: leadership, discernment, exhortation, teaching and pastor/shepherd.

Priorities

Shepherd Leaders (50%)

1. Huddle with leaders three times a year (March, August, and November).
2. Meet one-on-one with leaders three to four times a year.
3. Equip and develop each leader around our six leader essentials.
4. Monitor the health, effectiveness, and duration of groups.
5. Be available to minister and serve each leader.

Enlist Leaders (20%)

1. Interview all new leaders in preparation for each GroupLink.
2. Identify leader apprentices and begin development process.
3. Constantly recruit new leaders.

Oversee Multiplication (10%)

1. Track group progress through eighteen- to twenty-four-month duration.
2. Identify apprentice(s) enlistment at least six months before multiplication date.
3. Ensure timely multiplication of all groups.

Administration (15%)

1. Oversee the biannual update of group data.
2. Ensure timely follow-up after each leader huddle.

3. Contact each Starter Group to determine which groups are continuing into community groups.

4. Verify that all group information is current and accurate.

Training Events (5%)

1. Assist in Spring Training and Fall Retreat implementation, as needed.

2. Participate and serve at Community Group Leader Orientations, as needed.

3. Participate in "tool development," as needed.

4. Participate in GroupLink events.

5. Participate in other ministry-specific events.

appendix B
COMMUNITY GROUPS LEADER POSITION DESCRIPTION

Purpose

Community Group Leaders are responsible for providing their groups with vision, direction, and support. They primarily serve as shepherds by facilitating and monitoring their groups.

Qualifications

1. *Connected*. They have partnered with North Point through membership.
2. *Culture*. They embrace North Point's groups strategy and values.
3. *Character*. They are known for their integrity by those who know them best.

4. *Chemistry*. They have interviewed with a Groups Director.

5. *Competence*. They have previously participated in a small group.

Priorities

1. Shepherd the group by facilitating the group and monitoring its health.

2. Guide decisions relating to the covenant and curriculum around the three vital relationships.

3. Meet with Groups Director for one-on-one discussions at least three times a year, and for leader huddles three times a year.

4. Attend spring and fall training events.

5. Communicate updated group information to ministry office.

COMMUNITY GROUP COVENANT

Purpose

To provide a predictable environment where participants experience authentic community and spiritual growth.

Values & Goals

Relationships

While prayer and discussion of curriculum are key elements of a community group, the driving force behind the group is the building of relationships.

Authenticity

The atmosphere of a community group should encourage openness and transparency among members. This is an environment where people should feel free to be themselves.

Confidentiality
For authenticity to occur, members must be able to trust that issues discussed within a community group will not be shared outside the group.

Respect
Group members should never say anything that will embarrass their spouse or members of the group.

Availability
A primary responsibility of community is to prioritize for specific relationships. This requires a willingness to be available to meet each other's needs.

Multiplication
Group members recognize that one of the goals of their group is to start a new group within eighteen to twenty-four months. This allows others to experience the community group relationship.

Group Guidelines
1. The group will meet from _____ through _____.
2. The group will meet on _____ night.
3. The group sessions will begin at _____ and end at _____.
4. The group time will typically consist of _____

minutes of sharing, _____ of study/discussion, and _____ of prayer.

5. The group will be a closed group until all members agree to additional members.
6. Group members will attend and participate on a regular basis. Members agree to pray for other group members on a weekly basis.

I covenant together with the other members of this group to honor this agreement.

Group Leader(s):
sign:

_____

_____

Group Members:

_____

_____

_____

_____

_____

_____

appendix D
COMMUNITY GROUP WINS

For the Group Members
- When group members are pursuing growth in the three vital relationships.

For the Group Leaders
- When they pursue growth in the three vital relationships.
- When they shepherd group members' growth in the three vital relationships.
- When they create a predictable small-group environment by successfully executing the six leader essentials.

For the Group Directors

- When they pursue growth in the three vital relationships.
- When they shepherd the leader's growth in the three vital relationships.
- When they equip the leader to shepherd group members' growth in the three vital relationships.
- When they equip the leader to create a predictable environment by successfully executing the six leader essentials.

appendix E
CHILDCARE REIMBURSEMENT POLICY

1. Reimbursement forms are available through the group leader or at a campus information table.
2. Forms are sequentially numbered for auditing purposes and, therefore, may not be duplicated.
3. Parents are reimbursed at a set rate for the cost of an individual babysitter (see reimbursement form for rates).
4. Individual forms are to be filled out after each group meeting by each family requesting reimbursement.
5. Group members are to return completed forms to the Groups Ministry office or a campus information table on Sundays.
6. Each form must be submitted within thirty (30) days of the group meeting.
7. Checks are issued and mailed within two weeks of receipt of request.

CHILDCARE REIMBURSEMENT FORM

NORTH POINT
COMMUNITY CHURCH
4350 North Point Parkway
Alpharetta, Georgia 30022
(o)770.290.5600 (f) 770.290.5601

No._____

Reimbursement Payable To:

Name _____

Address _____

City _____ State _____

Zip _____ Phone # _____

Group Leader Name _____

Childcare Reimbursement

Office Use Only

Today's Date: _____

Requested By: _____

Department: _____

Please fill out ONE form per event.
Form must be submitted within 30 days of event.

Account Number	Ministry Area Event (Area Fellowship, Community Group, Starting Point, Crown etc.)	Date	# of Children	# of Hours	Amount
1155-01-10-080					

For individual sitters, please use the chart below.

Individual Reimbursement Chart

Number of Children	Hours of Event			
	1	2	3	4
1	$ 7.00	$ 14.00	$ 21.00	$ 28.00
2	$ 7.50	$ 15.00	$ 22.50	$ 30.00
3	$ 8.00	$ 16.00	$ 24.00	$ 32.00
4	$ 8.50	$ 17.00	$ 25.50	$ 34.00

Group sitting of 5 or more children will be paid at a rate of $9 per hour.

Please mail or fax this form to the attention of the Community Groups Ministry

NOTES

1. "Awards and Accolades," www.starbucks.com. www.starbucks.com/aboutus/recognition.asp (accessed April 2004).

2. Scott Cook, "The Cultural Significance of the American Front Porch," *The Evolution of the American Front Porch*, http://xroads.virginia.edu/~CLASS/am483_97/projects/cook/cultur.html, as quoted in Joseph R. Myers, *The Search to Belong: Rethinking Intimacy, Community, and Small Groups* (Grand Rapids, MI: Zondervan, 2003), 120.

3. George Gallup Jr., *The People's Religion* (New York: MacMillan, 1989).

4. Phillip Langdon, *A Better Place to Live: Reshaping the American Suburb* (New York: HarperPerennial, 1994), as quoted in Randy Frazee, *The Connecting Church* (Grand Rapids, MI: Zondervan, 2001), 24.

5. John Ortberg, *Everybody's Normal till You Get to Know Them* (Grand Rapids MI: Zondervan, 2003), 30.

6. Randy Frazee, *Making Room for Life* (Grand Rapids, MI: Zondervan, 2003), 33.

7. Genesis 1:31.

8. Ortberg, *Everybody's Normal*, 31–32.

9. Ephesians 6:12.

10. Ortberg, *Everybody's Normal*, 33.

11. Henry Cloud, *Changes That Heal* (Grand Rapids, MI: Zondervan, 2003), 54.

12. Ortberg, *Everybody's Normal*, 47.

13. Bill Donahue and Russ Robinson, *Building a Church of Small Groups* (Grand Rapids, MI: Zondervan, 2001), 29.

14. John 17:11.

15. Ibid., 40.

16. John 13:34–35.

17. Francis Schaeffer, *The Mark of a Christian* (Downers Grove, IL: InterVarsity Press, 1970), 14–15.

18. Frazee, *Making Room for Life*, 35.

19. John 3:16.

20. 2 Samuel 11.

21. Joshua 8.

22. James 1:22.

23. Matthew 22:37–40.

24. Hebrews 10:24–25.

25. Andy Stanley, Reggie Joiner, and Lane Jones, *7 Practices of Effective Ministry* (Sisters, OR: Multnomah, 2004), 87–88.

26. *American Heritage Dictionary of the English Language: Fourth Edition,* 2000, s.v. "strategy."

27. Exodus 18:14–23

28. John Eldredge, *Waking the Dead* (Nashville, TN: Thomas Nelson, 2003), 193.

29. Stanley, Joiner, and Jones, *7 Practices,* 89.

30. Ibid., 122.

31. Larry Crabb, as quoted in Frazee, *The Connecting Church,* 13.

"Andy Stanley offers a fresh perspective on ageless truths that will be of enormous benefit to today's leaders and to future generations."
— Patrick S. Flood, chairman and CEO, HomeBanc Mortgage Corporation

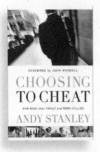

CHOOSING TO CHEAT
Choosing to Cheat presents a strategic plan for resolving the tension between work and home—reversing the destructive pattern of giving to your company and career what belongs to your family.
1-59052-329-6

HOW GOOD IS GOOD ENOUGH?
Goodness is not even a requirement to enter God's kingdom—thankfully, because we'll never be good enough. And Christianity is beyond fair—it's merciful. Find out why Jesus taught that goodness is not even a requirement to enter heaven—and why Christianity is beyond fair.
1-59052-274-5

THE NEXT GENERATION LEADER
Be the kind of leader you'd admire! Find inspiration, encouragement, and proven advice from pastor and bestselling author Andy Stanley.
1-59052-046-7

VISIONEERING
Andy Stanley shows readers how to set goals and obliterate the obstacles to a passionately-lived, meaningful life. He offers a workable plan for discovering a life vision aligned with God's own vision.
1-57673-787-X

DON'T MISS THESE ADDITIONAL MINISTRY TOOLS FROM
ANDY STANLEY AND NORTHPOINT RESOURCES!

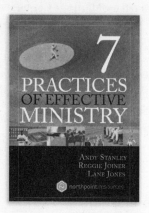

7 PRACTICES OF EFFECTIVE MINISTRY

Bestselling author Andy Stanley is joined by two respected ministry specialists to give pastors an insightful and entertaining parable for every church leader who yearns for a more simplified approach to ministry.

ISBN: 1-59052-373-3

DISCOVERING GOD'S WILL STUDY GUIDE

Designed for small groups or personal study, this companion study guide to the *Discovering God's Will DVD* will take readers through the important steps of decision making.

ISBN: 1-59052-379-2

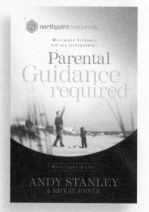

PARENTAL GUIDANCE REQUIRED STUDY GUIDE

This six-session companion study guide to the *Parental Guidance Required DVD* is a practical resource that will encourage parents to closely examine the relationships in their child's life.

ISBN: 1-59052-381-4